100 Ways to Annoy Your Guests

What every hotelier needs to avoid

Peter J Venison CVO

Clink
Street

London | New York

Published by Clink Street Publishing 2020

Copyright © 2020

First edition.

ISBN: 978-1-913568-86-3 – Paperback
978-1-913568-87-0 – Ebook

To my four children, Sue, Simon, Sarah-Kate and Jonathan,
of whom I am all immensely proud.

Also by Peter Venison

Managing Hotels
Heinemann Professional Publishing (London), 1983.
Reprinted 1984,1986,1988

100 Tips for Hoteliers
iUniverrse, 2005

In the Shadow of the Sun
iUniverse, 2005

Out of the Shadow of the Sun
Clink Street Publishing, 2020

Contents

Preface

For most of my working life I was involved in the management of hotels or the management of managers managing hotels. Much of this work involved the practicalities of keeping operations working smoothly and profitably. From an operational point of view, this involved the management of people, the supply and control of goods and materials, the control of the costs, the accounting and cash management, the return on investment, the promotion and advertising of the enterprise, the design and construction of the facilities and so on. I was concerned about getting the best possible performance out of the personnel and I wanted to be running a company for whom people liked to work. Naturally, I was concerned about the product we were offering and realised that, without satisfying our guests, there would be no business.

However, in retrospect, I spent far more time on managing the enterprise than experiencing its end result, i.e. the service and value that we offered. Since my retirement I have moved my focus from managing hotels to experiencing them. This experience has often been amazing, but, more often than not, has been disappointing. I have become a hotel guest rather than a hotel manager and this booklet is written from that standpoint, even though its prime audience will be hotel managers and students and teachers in the hospitality industry. I have not attempted to explore how to get things done in any depth; I have simply tried to highlight why they need doing.

To manage a hotel does not require a brilliant mind nor an amazing academic brain. It is not a science, nor does it require outstanding artistic ability. It does require a good deal of common sense and an ability to organise, to lead, to look and see. It is not for the lazy, although its comfortable surroundings can lead to this. It requires constant vigilance; otherwise the high standards set will slip away. Your customers might notice this before you do.

There are so many points of contact between members of hotel staff and the customer; so many places where things can go well or badly. But, to correct the annoyances and irritations heaped upon the hotel guest, we first need to recognise them. This book attempts to do just that; it does not go into the detail of how they are eliminated, but, taken individually, with the exception of a few that have been built into the hardware, each and every one of them can be easily eradicated with a little thought and effort. The first step for any hotel manager in this regard is to recognise that these simple deficiencies do exist and, hopefully, this little book will be a helpful aid in their eradication.

A hundred things that will definitely annoy your guests

1. Unclear or misleading directional instructions

2. Badly lit, sited and unclear signage

3. Confusing welcome signage at airport

4. Uncomfortable, cramped, transfer vehicle

5. Untidy, unkempt, and potholed driveway

6. Unsightly view of staff quarters, loading bays, administration office en route to the hotel entrance

7. Priority parking spaces for hotel management

8. Long lines at check-in desk

9. Too much form filling at check in

10. Disinterested receptionists

11. Failure to recognise or acknowledge a returning guest

12. An untidy dumping ground behind front desk

13. Poor directions to rooms

14. Illegible, badly lit elevator buttons and directional signs

15. Staff chasing tips

16. Faulty room key cards

17. Slow luggage delivery

18. Insufficient in-room luggage storage space and no luggage rack

19. Uncomfortable beds...

20. ... and uncomfortable pillows

21. Badly made beds

22. Ineffective turn down service

23. 'No steal' clothes hangers and unusable hanging rails

24. Insufficient space or light in closets

25. Complicated safe instructions

26. Badly positioned, dark, in-room safes

27. Poor/expensive laundry service

28. Room furniture not fit for use

29. Inadequate drawer space

30. Useless bedside tables

31. Unreadable air conditioning controls

32. Noisy air conditioner

33. Blasting air conditioning

34. Empty minibars

35. Overpriced minibars

36. Noisy minibars

37. Complicated room lighting controls

38. Excess of LED lights at night

39. Poor bed reading lights

40. Complicated TV controls

41. Inadequate television channels

42. Noisy neighbours/ thin walls

43. Too much corridor noise

44. Inadequate, awkwardly sited electrical sockets

45. Poor Wi-Fi connections and overcharging

46. Complicated telephone systems

47. Useless telephone operational instructions

48. Fast track service that isn't

49. Complicated shower controls

50. Slippery tub showers

51. Inadequate bathroom lighting

52. Inadequate bathroom shelf space

53. Strange bathroom layouts

54. Inadequate or inappropriate in room/bathroom glasses

55. Uncontrollable and variable water temperature

56. Dirt under vanity shelves or behind doors

57. Lack of facecloths

58. Unreadable amenities

59. Unopenable soap

60. Toilet paper in unreachable spot

61. Room service trays in corridors for too long

62. Inappropriate and intrusive music

63. Untidy lobbies

64. Noisy lobbies

65. Snooty concierges

66. Inappropriate range of stock in shop

67. Overpricing in shop

68. Failure to control opening times of hotel shops

69. Banquet room left untidy

70. Poorly lit banquet/ meeting rooms

71. Noisy banquet rooms

72. Unsociable banquet tables

73. Ill-equipped breakfast buffets

74. Pre-cooked, tired looking, buffet food

75. Not enough fresh produce on buffet

76. Lack of management presence at breakfast

77. Inadequate supply of crockery/cutlery at breakfast

78. Traffic jam at the toast and coffee machines

79. Poor restaurant table lay-outs

80. Repetitive resort menus

81. Inflexible menu ordering policy

82. Hot food that is not

83. Overpriced wine lists

84. No space in restaurant for hotel guests

85. No nibbles at the bar

86. Unsociable furniture lay out in bar

87. Unfriendly barman

88. Untidy gardens and grounds

89. Badly lit walkways

90. Unwashed vehicles

91. Overpriced car parks

92. Unsupervised pool areas

93. Insufficient pool towels

94. Insufficient pool loungers

95. Dirty beach

96. Beach vendors

97. Evening turndown service at 2 pm

98. Impatient knocking at the door

99. Unavailable or unseen hotel manager

100. Unavailable or unseen assistant manager

"It was almost impossible to find the place. I had driven two hundred miles and I was tired. There were no signs to tell me where the entrance was and my satnav took me into the supermarket car park. I was very irate when I finally found it."

– MR DONALD LOSTIT, MANCHESTER, UK

"There were potholes all the way up the driveway. Can you believe that? A five-star hotel with a driveway like the I.95."

– JIMMY CARTER, QUEENS, NY

"There was no place to park, but I noticed that the Manager had a special place right next to the front door. That doesn't seem right, does it?"

– CLIVE NEAT, PERTH, AUSTRALIA

"I must have stayed in this hotel twenty times. I am more regular than the personnel at the front desk. That's probably why they always ask me if I've stayed before. You would think someone would teach them to google. I really don't know why I stay here because it certainly doesn't feel like home."

– MR STEVE LONGROAD, AUSTIN, TEXAS

"It's time you changed your key card system. Every time I get to my room the thing gives me the red light, so I have to go all the way back to the lobby to get another one. Sometimes it doesn't work twice in a row. It is very annoying and if you don't fix it, I am going to give the red light to you."

– 'FRUSTRATED', TEL AVIV

Chapter One
The Arrival

The arrival experience at a hotel, although seemingly routine, can cause stress levels to rise. Have I come to the right place? I hope they still have my reservation. Where will I park? Even frequent travellers are on alert during the arrival process. First impressions are extremely important. Arriving guests have a very high level of expectancy. For frequent users it is like coming to a second home – but only if they are given a welcome homecoming. For many guests, going to a hotel can be a special occasion, one they have been looking forward to or saved up for. They will have high hopes; the arrival experience is not the place to dash those. The more you upset the guest on arrival, the harder you will have to work at recovery. Here are some ways you can annoy and disappoint your guests before they have even reached their room.

1. Make it hard to find

Just getting to a hotel can be a frustrating experience. By definition most hotel guests are from out of town and, therefore, in unfamiliar territory. You, the Manager, of course, know exactly where your hotel is located, but your guests, particularly first-time guests, do not. Put yourself in their driving seat. Is the entrance to your hotel clearly marked? Is there adequate warning to drivers that they will need to make a turn soon? Is the entry sign large enough to be read from the road at normal driving speed and is it well-lit enough to be clear at night?

If the guest is finding you by satnav, have you tested the instructions yourself to make sure that they are correct? You will really annoy your guest if the satnav is asking them to turn into a farmyard or supermarket car park.

In city addresses, with the likelihood of heavy traffic outside your door, is your signage large enough and illuminated enough for an out of town driver to see from a distance, so that he can prepare (and warn others) that he is going to slow down? There is nothing more annoying in a strange town than driving past your hotel due to inadequate signage and having to drive around an unfamiliar block.

If your guests are arriving by plane and being met at the airport, make sure that the greetings sign is clear and professionally produced. Hotels often subcontract the airport/railway station greeting and transfer to a third-party operator. Sometimes these companies' greetings signs are touting their name rather than that of your hotel. This can be confusing to an arriving passenger, peering into a sea of signs and faces. Remember, your arriving guest will probably have just been through the frustrating (and, to some, frightening) process of immigration, luggage retrieval, and so on. If possible, get your greeter to hold a sign with your hotel name clearly displayed. Hotels that have not subcontracted this task and are using their own people, properly uniformed as such, will clearly be following best practice.

Finally, there is the actual vehicle with which you transfer your guests from airport to hotel. Management must be sure that suitable vehicles are being utilised and that they are being parked at the airport or station in a spot that has easy access for your guests. Make sure that they will not have to push or pull their luggage over kerbs or ramps and minimise the amount of traffic dodging they may be required to do. Train your drivers to assist them with the bags. Remember, this collection and delivery process is the first real contact your guest will have with your product. A dirty, uncomfortable, cramped vehicle with poor luggage space, and an uncommunicative driver will be a very poor start in your relationship with your new guest. This is your first chance to impress; it is also your first potential pitfall because a hectic foreign airport or railway station can be a traumatic place for many people. When you, the Manager, arrive back in town from a trip, don't opt for special chauffeured treatment; try the system that your guests do.

2. Outer appearance

How tidy is the approach to your hotel and what does it look like from the outside? Remember that the first impression a guest will have will be what he sees from the outside, whether he is arriving by car, bus or bike. When your hotel was designed the architect probably gave considerable thought to the arrival 'impression'. Is the integrity of his plan still intact? Go outside and look, both in the day and in the dark. Does the arrival experience incorporate views of the staff quarters, or the loading bay, or the garbage? If so, it would be the equivalent of inviting someone into your home, not through the front door, but through the back alley. When a guest arrives and steps out of her car, can she see into your administrative offices, with their flip charts, overflowing wastepaper bins, electric wires at the back of computers and so on? So often, an arrival experience is spoiled by unnecessary and completely avoidable views of the back of house. And be aware that this untidy state of affairs is more pronounced at night when the lights of empty offices shine bright.

When the architect designed the hotel his renderings and plans would probably have shown the unfurnished product. Now that it is operational take a new look at how it appears with furnishings. From outside, looking up, do the drapes look a mess? Are you looking at the underside of furniture? Are there all sorts of masts or aerials spoiling the clean line roof profile? Is the planned floodlighting of the building still functioning? If you have flags flying, are they still in good condition?

I can tell you how upset I was a few years ago when visiting the beautiful town of Plettenburg Bay, South Africa, to see in the distance the striking building of the Beacon Isle hotel. This hotel, back in the early 1970s had been designed as a striking piece of modern architecture with crisp clean lines and curves. It was remarkable for its simplicity. It stood out as a symbol of modernism against one of the most beautiful land and seascapes in the world. To my horror, since I was last there several years before, Management had allowed the clean roof line to be ruined with several unplanned structures and masts, which completely ruined the pristine intention of the architect. A lot of time, thought and expertise is often put into the planning and design of a hotel; management should respect that.

Arriving at a hotel can be made into an adventure or experience. It should also be a 'discovery', which will be memorable. I remember the arrival at the Earth Lodge, a safari hotel in Sabi Sands, Africa. Having followed little wooden direction signs down a dirt road for about ten miles, I started to wonder where on earth I was going. Finally, the signs stopped next to a grassy mound in the bush, where the message carved on the sign asked one to call a number for 'reception'. There was no building in sight, so the idea that you were at the reception seemed ridiculous. I dialled the number and, after maybe a minute, a Land Cruiser appeared, driven by a ranger. He jumped out, welcomed us to the Lodge and asked us to follow him, leaving our vehicle, our luggage and the Land Cruiser behind. We walked down a gentle slope behind the mound, until we were in a hollow about six feet deep. In front of us, suddenly, were two carved but unobtrusive wooden doors, which sprung open as we approached to reveal a beautiful vista. Lo and behold we were in the open-air lobby of a wonderful game lodge, looking at a waterhole surrounded by game – none of which had been visible from the arrival mound due to the clever way the architect had used the contours of the land. And what a lovely surprise it was!

Clearly there are not many hotels that can be made to disappear and then reappear to give arriving guests a pleasant surprise, but a sense of discovery upon arrival can often be achieved by such devices at bends in the driveway, planting, pieces of sculpture or other artwork. Take a look at your arrival route. Maybe, with some thought, it could be improved. Even if the scope in this way is limited, the installation of something unique at the porte cochere, such as a piece of sculpture or a fountain, at least lifts an otherwise purely functional space into an interesting and welcoming one.

Directional signage within your grounds is also important for a guest who is driving. Remember, the driver has probably driven a long distance and may be tired, or is driving an unfamiliar rental vehicle. He will not be in the mood for following imprecise and confusing direction signs. For example, quite frequently a sign for parking will be pointing in a different direction from a sign for 'registration'. Go and check the signage in your grounds; imaging that it is your first visit. Does it all make sense?

When guests arrive in a vehicle at your front door, give them time. Don't rush them out of their vehicle. Remember, they may have driven a long way. They may not be perfectly organised in regard to which bags they want brought out of the car and which could be left. They may be clutching maps or books or bags full of trash from the journey. Give them a moment to collect their themselves and their thoughts. Being hustled and hassled by a porter at the door can be irritating. Asking a guest, arriving in a taxi, clutching a suitcase and a hanging bag, "Are you checking in, sir?" is redundant.

Above all, remember that if your hotel looks like a mess from the outside this could be the view that you have got used to and accepted. It is, however, a view that will be sending negative signals to your guests, who may be seeing it for the first time. If you really want to annoy your guests before they have stepped through the door, park your car outside the front door in a spot marked 'Reserved for General Manager'. And if that doesn't do it, make sure that they have to go hunting for trolleys or help with the bags.

3. Registration

Registration. What a terrible word! Asking someone to 'register' has shades of signing onto the National Health Service or the tax registry. You should not be asking your customers to 'register', you should be offering them a warm and genuine welcome or, if you prefer, reception. Most hotel registration desks are not desks; they are counters, such as you would find in a bank or a post office, the only difference being the lack of metal grids. A counter is a barrier. It may be necessary but, just at the point of 'welcome' your guest is confronted with a barrier. Can you imagine asking your guests at home to pass through a turnstile to get into your hallway? A lower desk at which an arrival can be seated to sign in, as many hotels offer, is far more friendly. However, if this is just not practical, at least, have the receptionist walk around the barrier, once the formalities are done, to hand the key to the arriving guest. Just a simple gesture like that demonstrates warmth, and you absolutely want your arriving guests to 'feel the warmth'.

However, the first question often asked by the receptionist is 'Do you have a reservation?' That is a bit like the dentist's receptionist asking you if you have come about your teeth. The chances that the arrival does not have a reservation are very slim and, should that be the case, they will quickly tell you.

"Welcome to our hotel. May I have your name please?" would be a better first approach. After that it should be plain sailing because, with modern technology, as soon as you have noted a name, a tsunami of reservation requests and guest history should be instantly available, leading immediately to, if appropriate, a "Welcome back Mr X." Nothing is more stress reducing or appreciated than a "Welcome back!"

On the other hand, "Have you stayed here before?" is a real downer if you have. "They don't remember me. I'm obviously not important to them. They don't really CARE about me" and so on. This is the one question designed to annoy your repeat customer more than any other. Similarly, receptionists should be careful not to welcome someone back if they have never stayed before. This smacks of insincerity. "Oh, they just say that to everyone. We are all numbers to them." It is not a bad idea, if capacity allows, to operate a policy of upgrading repeat customers from time to time. It is something that really pleases frequent guests, as long as you make sure that they understand that you will not always be able to do so. Sometimes you will find that your upgraded guest gets to like the extra comfort and, on the next visit, is willing to pay the extra rate.

The next dissatisfaction hotspot is a line to check-in. Hopefully this only occurs in your hotel on very rare occasions. If it is so frequent that you resort to ropes and poles, then you are clearly understaffed, even if only at peak times. Having travelled to get to you, probably enduring lines elsewhere, the last thing your arriving guest needs to find is that she is obliged to join another line, particularly if you are demonstrating with your ropes and poles that it happens often. The removal of this annoyance is entirely within the control of management through the judicious use of personnel and resources.

Then there is the obligatory registration form. Often this is full of information that no arrival actually reads or is asking questions that have already been answered at the time of reservation. Most of these forms are throwbacks to the time that governments or the police insisted on the collection of this information before hotels had the capability of storing it online. Ask yourself, why are we asking people to read and sign off? Is this not bureaucratic overkill? Take a moment to read over your check-in documentation and eliminate the duplication or unnecessary. Checking in to a hotel should not be akin to applying for unemployment compensation.

If your hotel can only function at check in with a stand-up desk then take a moment to 'check-in' yourself. What can you see whilst the desk clerk is going through the process of the paperwork? Probably a load of clutter! The area behind the front desk and the facing wall should not a dumping ground for deliveries, laundry returns, or the receptionists' lunch. Whilst recognising that it is a working space with a clear function, it should not become the storage place for anything that needs to be delivered. It also should not provide views into a chaotic looking office behind. Who wants to see the Assistant Manager, in his shirtsleeves with his feet on the desk? Who wants to see posters and memos that make the place look like your kitchen fridge? You are not operating a post office! Remember, somebody put thought into designing this area so that it was pleasing to the eye and a reflection of the style and quality of the establishment. Don't allow it to be spoiled. It is so easy to get used to untidiness behind the front desk if you work there. Mess becomes the norm and you just don't see it anymore. Your arriving guest does!

Body language is very important. The receptionist who persistently looks down at a computer screen, whilst simultaneously talking to the arriving guest is not as customer friendly as one who looks her in the eye with a warm smile. Nor is the clerk who, whilst 'welcoming' a guest, continues to discuss her private business with a colleague. "I don't really care what you did last night or what you intend to so this evening. Concentrate on me. Please." Make sure that your receptionists are trained to ask welcoming questions that show a personal interest. "Have your travelled far today, sir?" "Oh, I see you come from London; I would love to go there one day. It must be so nice" and so on.

Imparting necessary information to the arriving guest is important, but not too much. Attempting to recite the entire guest information book at check-in is a waste of time because the arriving guest simply wants to get to their room and will not be listening. But, a simple question like, "Do you have any special needs?" or "Would you like a newspaper delivered in the morning?" will show that the hotel CARES about you. Review with your staff what are the key pieces of information that are important for a guest to know at the time of check-in and set the limit.

One could say, "Why bother with reception clerks in this technological age?" Many hotels are moving towards self-check-in by machine, on the theory that this saves guest time and staff costs. It may well be the proof required that the registration form required at check in is redundant, but it ignores the benefit of human interaction. The arrival process is one of the few opportunities the hotelier has to personally interact with the guest. Hotel guests remember their stay in hotels favourably by the kindness, help, and attitude of the staff, not by interaction with inanimate objects. That is why gestures such as welcome drinks, or leis, or other friendly gifts, work so well. They set out to show that Management CARE and that they value your business. But, be careful not to insult them by offering liquid gunge to drink. If you are going to offer a welcome drink, make sure it is a 'real' drink, not just a sweet mixture from a plastic bottle. If the arrivals are not in a group, why not ask them what they would like to drink on the house? You can bet that many will say 'water'. Carried out effectively, the check-in process is a huge opportunity to score points with the guest. However, if you want to annoy your guests before they have even reached their room, through cold and indifferent behaviour or systems, the front desk is a great place to start.

4. Finding your room

The guest's first trip to their room can be an adventure. Remember, that, unless they are extremely regular guests, they will not be familiar with the geography of the hotel. If they are not being accompanied to the room by a member of staff, which would be preferable, they will be following verbal instructions from the desk clerk or a printed map or some sort as a helpful handout. The most important pieces of information an arriving guest needs are, of course, the room number and floor. Armed with this, specific rooms ought to be easy to find, provided that the guest has located the right wing of the hotel or the appropriate elevator, and that the directional arrows on the signs are clear, and that the luggage trolley can negotiate the bumps and turns of the route. Also, take a fresh look at your elevators. Are the elevator buttons clearly marked or is their shorthand a bit of a puzzle to first time users? For example, does 'G' mean 'ground' or 'garage'? If 'L' means 'lobby', what does 'LL' mean? Is there enough light in the cabin to actually see the buttons or do your guests have to take out their cell phone torches? Piped music started in elevators; is yours still relevant and/or is it too loud? (Remember, that loud music from an elevator wafts down the bedroom corridors every time the doors open on a floor. Have you ever been allocated a room next to the elevator bank?) And is there room enough in the elevator for your party and the luggage porter? Who could imagine how many opportunities there are to annoy your guests just in one elevator?

5. Who gets the tip?

When I was a desk clerk at a London hotel in the 1960s, there were many Arabian sheiks staying as guests of international oil companies, whilst drilling was taking place in search of oil in their homelands. They had come from the desert and were unsophisticated in the ways of Western society, particularly as it applied to luxury Mayfair hotels. The money they were using came in a plentiful supply from 'Big Oil', and so, using it to tip the staff was no hardship. Our room keys were too heavy and bulky to conveniently fit in a dish dash, so were handed in to the desk clerks every time a sheikh left the hotel. Likewise, on their return, they were handed back, only this time the clerk's hand would hover long enough for a tip. I got paid £8 per week. Each time I handed a key out to a sheikh, I got, at least, the smallest note – £5 and sometimes even a tenner. Naturally, we clerks, rotated the hand back task. There was plenty to go around. Life at front and concierge desks has not changed. Where there is an arrival, there is a tip. The question is, who gets it? And how annoying it can be for the arriving guest if everyone seems to want it. Is it the porter who takes your car keys and, maybe, your luggage out the trunk? Is it the porter who brings said luggage to your room? Is it the reception clerk who has accompanied you to the room and explained how to turn the lights on? Or is it all or none of the above? The constant and repetitive outstretched palm during the check-in process can be aggravating. As a manager, recognise this, and set some rules.

6. Key cards

There are many advantages to electronic key cards but they are a real pain when they don't work. There is nothing more annoying in a hotel than having to wend your way back to the lobby from your room when the red light at the door just won't turn green, however many times you put it in the slot. If this happens frequently, then there is clearly something wrong with your system and it needs to be corrected. How would you know? Ask your desk clerks to maintain a written record of every time they have had to reboot a key. You will see a pattern emerge. Correct it. At the same time discontinue the practice of cutting off the key function after a guest has stayed a few days, without advising him that you are doing so. And, whilst you are at it, get rid of those tacky adverts that grace many key cards and replace them with useful information that the guest might need in regard to your hotel.

7. Explaining the room features

When a member of staff accompanies a guest to their room upon arrival, they can perform a useful service. En route, much of the information overload that should not be communicated at the front desk, can be imparted before reaching the room. Once there, only the fundamental and necessary functions of the room should be explained because what the arriving guest probably wants you to do is leave, so that she can go to the bathroom or just relax after the journey. There is a fine line between the 'need to know' and the 'could know'. At this point, need to know might be the better option. A good manager should almost script the room facility description for the receptionist or porter, so that just the right and appropriate information is imparted. Phrases like, "Here is the bathroom" are redundant. If the staff member who is showing a guest to her room is also handling the luggage, then he should assist with the sensible distribution of it within the room, not just dump it at the door.

Many hotel guests, upon first arrival in their allocated room will head straight to the window to see the view. How this is handled by the accompanying receptionist or porter must depend upon the quality of the view, which will obviously not be the same in all rooms. If the view is excellent or reasonable it probably makes sense to train your staff to head straight to the window to 'demonstrate' it and to point out any items of interest. This way will get them off to a good start before explaining how the rest of the room works.

Finally, if it is your policy to leave a welcome gift, make sure that it is either consumable, preferably during the guests visit, or extremely useful. Most of your customers will not want cheap memorabilia to add to their collection or the weight of their luggage, nor will they want a bottle of cheap undrinkable red wine with no corkscrew. China Airlines used to give out cheap plastic combs; Concorde passengers used to get silver plated items that they could actually keep and use, which every time they did, reminded them of their trip.

8. Where is my luggage?

When a guest, as many do, is relying on luggage to be delivered to the room, she is expecting that to occur close to the time that she arrives or is escorted to the room. Ideally, the luggage porter will be waiting at the door of the room when the guest reaches it. If you are marooned in your room awaiting the arrival of your luggage, every minute seems like half an hour. You know that if you go to the bathroom there will be a knock at the door, so you wait. Eventually you call down to the front desk with a plaintive query, "What has happened to my luggage?" Normally the answer is, "It's on its way", even if it isn't. When the porter does show up with the bags he now has the chance to redeem himself but, more often than not, he simply plonks the bags down and leaves, (with or without a tip), without thought as to where best to place the cases or even to remove the luggage rack from the closet, assuming that there is one available. It is very annoying to hotel guests that hotel rooms have often not been designed with any consideration as to where luggage can be placed, so it is most helpful when a porter stops to configure the best arrangement for you, even if that extends to an offer to go in search of an additional luggage rack. It is quite probable that luggage porters are not long-term employees. It seems a fairly menial job, but like all others in the front line with the guests, it is an extremely impactful one. Let your porters know that they are important cogs in the wheel of the hotel. Treat them with respect and train them to do the job just as you would like them to do it.

"The air conditioning system in the room was awful. It rattled whenever it switched on and blasted at me in bed. When I turned it off, the room became like an oven. I broke my finger nail trying to open the window, which I couldn't. The air conditioning control thingy was useless. I shall never stay at this hotel again."

– GILLIAN FROST, MEMPHIS

"Please move the safe in the room to a place where I can see into it. And while you are at it, get rid of that black felt lining; you can't see anything in this little black hole!"

– LADY ANNE D'ARCY, STOW-ON-THE-WOLD, UK

"My pet peeve in your hotels is the hangers in the closet. They have got silly little eyes and slots, instead of hooks. It is very annoying when you try to hang up your clothes. You need three pairs of hands. Surely there is a better way to do this?"

– MRS JUNE HANGOUT, BOGNOR REGIS, UK

"Your beds are super comfortable. It is a pity that nobody has taught the staff how to make them!"

– SALLY SACH, GLASGOW, SCOTLAND

"Your hotel rooms are very noisy. You can hear everything that is going on in the next room; you don't need your own TV. At night, all I could hear were doors slamming and other guests shouting at each other down the hallway. I will not stay with you again."

– WILLY DRUMMOND, DES MOINES, USA

"Have you tried to read in bed in your hotel? The bedside lights are useless!"

– MR GEORGE BLINDER, CHICAGO, ILL.

Chapter Two
The Hotel Room

Hotel bedrooms and suites are the core of any hotel; in most cases they are the raison d'être. However, the word 'bedroom' is not strictly accurate because a hotel bedroom needs to be more than a place to sleep. It is also a place to work, eat and live in. Unfortunately, the actual bed or beds tend to dominate the room, so it is very important that the remaining space is used wisely. If hoteliers cannot provide a room that is fit for purpose then they will have failed. Obviously, different price levels and different clientele will demand different products and, since space relates heavily to costs, budget hotel rooms are obviously going to be smaller and less luxurious than those in five- star hotels.

A universal feature of hotel rooms is that the door to the hallway opens inwards and that the members of staff, who are likely to enter the room, normally have a key, unlike your front door at home. Many hotel employees seem to have mastered the knack of opening and entering the room, simultaneously with knocking. This can be very annoying and sometimes embarrassing. Staff should be taught to knock and wait for a response from within, then knock again, before entering.

Leading international hotel chains have been building thousands of hotel rooms since the first Holiday Inns and Hiltons came on stream and, to a large degree, they have massaged the product into something resembling efficiency and comfort. It would be hard to design a cookie cutter room to suit all hotels, primarily due to the fact that more expensive hotels will need to offer more in space and amenities, than budget ones. Also, even hotel chains offering standard products ("You'll get no surprises!") need to accommodate design variations as a result of the different specifications of the site, its topography, and other real estate aspects. It is, however, quite remarkable that, even after the building of thousands of hotel rooms, some design flaws keep re-occurring. Here are some of them.

1. The Bed

The bed is the most essential item in a hotel. Without beds, there is no point in having a hotel. It should, therefore, be the most important piece of furniture in the establishment. It is clear that this has been recognised by all successful hotel chains and the standard of beds and mattresses in most hotels has dramatically improved since this author started in the business. Beds have got larger and larger, as people's tastes in bed width have increased, but rooms have, if anything got smaller, causing a furniture crash. There is little point putting a king-size bed into a mini-size room, but this happens. It is also not acceptable to call a twin room such if two single beds have been pushed together, nor is it acceptable to sell a king bed when it is really two twins pushed together with a resultant ridge in the centre. A bad mattress is probably the most annoying thing that can befall a guest, followed closely by a bad pillow. Pillows are a very personal thing. Some guests like them hard, some like them soft, some like them thin, some like them plump, some like them with natural down, some artificial. Even, Her Majesty Queen Elizabeth, finds it necessary to travel with her own pillow! To accommodate this menu of pillow 'tastes', hotels must make a special effort, which could start by asking for a preference on the booking form but should continue by offering you options when you check-in.

However, it is not now often that the bed itself causes dissatisfaction in a hotel, but the way that the bed is made. There is almost a universal assumption made by hoteliers that all guests prefer a duvet to a blanket. This is not necessarily so and it can be quite an annoying and uphill battle with hotel staff to get rid of the duvet. Just as with the pillows, there should be choice, and that choice could start at the time of taking the booking. Under the guise of combating global warming and reducing laundry generated waste (and costs!), sheets are not often changed on a daily basis, other than for a change of occupant. This means that beds are 'remade' and, more often than not, rather badly. Sheets are not properly or tidily tucked in and the whole appearance can look like a teenager's bedroom. Housekeeping workers are often lowly paid and from modest personal surroundings. In their own home they almost certainly will not have the comforts of a hotel room – yet they are expected to reach a high level of housekeeping. Since the work of a chambermaid is carried out almost exclusively in the privacy of a hotel room it is a very difficult thing to supervise or quality check. High standards will only be achieved via training, inspection and correction. Every hotel manager should inspect, at random, at least ten bedrooms per day and, as is said elsewhere in this booklet, every manager should stay overnight in a different room of his hotel at least once per month, without prior notification to the housekeeping staff. That is the best way to suss out the rat's nests and the bumps.

2. The Closet

Very high up the scale of ways to annoy your guests is to provide them with those clothes hangers where the hook cannot be removed from the hanging rail. This is a way of saying, 'You are our valued guest, but – we don't trust you'. There must have been an army of hanger thieves targeting hotels, which prompted someone to invent these horrible user-unfriendly gizmos. It also causes the maximum annoyance just at the beginning of your guest's stay, as they are unpacking. Your guests get a welcome note from the manager and then a warning that they must not steal his hangers. This aggravation becomes a double whammy if, in order to save space, the hanging rail is at right angles to the closet door, forcing one to hang clothes, one behind the other, guaranteeing that it will be difficult for a guest to get hold of the clothes at the back. If there are two occupants in a room, one of them is going to have to hang their clothes in a completely inaccessible place. Guess which one?

And, why is it that there are never enough hangers in the closet upon arrival? This can be slightly irritating at first but can easily escalate into annoyance when one calls 'housekeeping' to request some more. Sometimes it seems as if you were asking for gold bars to be delivered.

Further 'closet irritation' is fuelled by the fact that, whoever worked out the ideal length of a closet did so before some other helpful company decided to provide ironing boards and irons for self-help guests. Where are the ironing boards stored? Of course, in the incredible shrinking closet, where they are yet another encroachment of the limited space. Well, your guests haven't even unpacked yet and they are already annoyed.

3. The Safe

The mini-safe; the afterthought of hotel room design. The operation of the in-room safe can be quite challenging, verging, sometimes, on annoying. Because they vary in design, one needs, before potentially jamming the thing up and having to call maintenance, to read the instructions. This can be really challenging for most people and almost impossible for older people with poor eyesight. The instructions are either too complicated or too small to read, and are often in a position to which is difficult to access. Alternatively, they are worn away, or are printed on a separate card, which is often missing. Naturally you want to get it right for fear of never seeing your valuables again, but when the safes are installed in places that are difficult to access, as they invariably are, proper safe operation can be a challenge. They are often installed too high for many people, or too low. Which lady, having dressed up for the evening wants to get down on hands and knees to recover her jewellery?

Then, of course, there is the size. If the safe is not big enough to take a ladies' handbag and a tablet, then it is annoyingly small, and quite useless. Finally, just to pour salt into the wound, why is it that in-room safes always seem to be lined with black material, which makes it very difficult to see inside?

4. The furniture

How a hotel bedroom is furnished depends, of course, on what type of hotel it is. Obviously, motels, with the majority of one-night stays, will need less storage space than, say, resort hotels. However, there are basic needs in this regard which need to be met. Clearly, every hotel bedroom, by definition, needs a bed. At minimum, it also needs a desk and/or table, two chairs, two bedside tables, and one or two luggage racks. This furniture needs to be capable of accommodating one or two guests' requirements to partake in a room service meal, work at a computer, watch the television (other than from a bed), or even engage in social activity, such as playing cards. So often the hotel room furniture is designed to satisfy one or other of these activities, but not all of them, with the result that two people, sharing a room service meal have to do so from different height chairs and/or tables. They finish up 'camping' in a hotel room. This is unsatisfactory and annoying. However, hotel rooms HAVE been designed so that the desk can double as a dining table (for two) and that an easy chair can be a sofa and so on. It is essential, before construction, that a fully furnished mock-up room is built, to be thoroughly critiqued for its functionality and comfort, not only from a guest perspective but also in regard to housekeeping and maintenance. It is astounding that, after so many years and so many constructed hotels, that the perfect hotel room furniture has yet to exist.

There are often not enough drawers in a hotel room and, sometimes, they are, rather annoyingly, too shallow or too narrow to use for clothing items that we all carry, such as sweaters, blouses, shirts etc. After all, who wants to place the Bible on one's underpants? Also, the bedside tables are often devoid of drawers. They are sometimes devoid of space on top. They should be designed with the capability of holding a lamp, a phone, a book, a clock and some items, such as watches, rings, jewellery, etc., which people tend to take off at night, whether these items are on top or in a drawer. Annoyingly most hotel bedside tables do not pass this test.

Storing of luggage can also be a challenge. Many single occupants tend to throw their cases onto a bed and operate out of the case, but most want to unpack somewhat, whilst still having easy access to a suitcase. Designing in this space is essential, but it is almost ignored in hotel planning. It is both annoying and impractical for hotel guests to be grovelling around on the floor trying to find their socks in a suitcase.

These basic requirements do not necessarily mean more space and more cost. In most cases they can be cleverly designed in a compact way, by properly utilising the space that exists or is planned.

5. The air conditioning

This comes very high on the annoyance scale. It is the norm, rather than the exception, that something about the air conditioning system in your room will be wrong. It will either be too noisy, to draughty, too hot, too cold, too intermittent or just too awful. But, to add insult to injury, it will be very difficult for the hotel guest to do anything about it because he will not be able to read, nor understand, the little box on the wall, with which he is supposed to be in control. These boxes have been designed for people with twenty-twenty eyesight, who have to be exactly the right height to see the miniature screen. The digital displays are mostly so faint that they cannot be read by normal humans, and even if they could, will not easily be understood due to the jargon or symbols used. What could be so difficult in designing a control box that is easy to read, easy to understand, and placed somewhere that all guests can access it?

Then, there is the problem of the intermittent gale which seems to follow one around the room, and particularly attacks you when our get into bed. Whilst this is switched on you are destined to spend the night, either with intermittent and noisy blasts of cold air aimed straight at your head – or sweat. Don't bother getting out of bed to open the window because, the chances are it will be fixed closed. How annoying is that?

This air conditioning system will either be from a centralised plant, which might make it difficult to control on an individual room basis, or an individual room unit, either mounted on the wall or through the window. Centralised systems are normally much quieter than the through the wall type, but the lack of individual control can be most annoying. In-room units are normally noisier and subject to guest tampering. The only way to minimise the nuisance value and efficiency of the in-room air conditioning is through effective and regular servicing. This is not something which generally excites hotel managers, but, boring as it might be, it is absolutely necessary to monitor carefully.

6.　The in-room bar

Most hotel rooms sport a minibar, which is really a mini-fridge. God knows why, because most of them are empty or contain a couple of bottles of the world's most expensive water. (Is this actually telling the guest that the water in the bathroom tap is not potable?) The main function of these almost empty minibars, it would seem, is to intermittently make a whirring noise in the night as they happily switch themselves on and off to cool their empty innards. Annoying? When space in a hotel room is at a premium why waste it with a noisy, empty, minibar?

If you are staying in a hotel with trusting management, then the chances are that the minibar will be stuffed with all sorts of mini-bottles; beers, soft drinks and, maybe, wine. This truly is handy, but beware of the price list. It is, to say the least, annoying to find that your whisky has been marked up eleven times from cost, particularly when there is rarely a suitable glass available in the room in which to drink it. Sipping 12-year-old scotch in the plastic mug from the bathroom is not ideal, especially when the only access to ice is a trip down the hall in your pjs, because the ice trays in the minibar have not been refilled or no longer exist.

How do you stop your guests from getting their own back by stealing half of the minibar stock as they check out? Well, that is simple. You annoy them again by asking them to wait at checkout whilst you send someone to audit their bar. Since most of your guests are not really minibar thieves, let alone users, the annoyance caused in holding them all back at the gate would seem counterproductive. Unhappiness is the last emotion you want a departing guest to take with him.

The other minibar invention, which demonstrates how little guests can be trusted, is the automatic charge system, when, if an item is lifted from its position on the shelf in the bar, the guest is charged. No lifting the little critter out to see exactly what it is. Touch it; you own it! What happened to the old Honour Bar?

Minibars are sometimes supplemented by a display of chocolates, nuts, biscuits and, occasionally, condoms. Although often very welcome and tempting, you can be sure that this appetising array of goodies is overpriced, and much of it can be rather stale. Whatever happened to good old room service? Finally, why is it that the minibar is so often situated so close to the floor that one has to practically get on hands and knees to find out what is in it. We don't install fridges in our kitchens at home at knee high level, so why do it in a hotel room?

7. The lighting

Sometimes, not much; sometimes too much. The lighting of a hotel can be a catastrophe. A constant battle rages between lighting to create a mood and lighting so that a guest can actually see. They need not be combatant. The first likely challenge with room illumination will be as you enter the room. Sometimes, pressing the obvious switch just inside the door will achieve nothing, and pressing the next one, the same. This will normally nudge the brain into concluding that there must be a slot somewhere to insert a card, presumably the same with which you have just opened the door (or, often any other card, like your gym membership). If this works, you are in business, and, hopefully, the room is now flooded with light. These card control systems were introduced to cut down on power usage whilst a room is unoccupied. I have yet to see any quantification of their effectiveness. Sometimes, card or no card, the switch at the door does not turn on the lights and, in this case, you will need to proceed around this unfamiliar room trolling for light switches or buttons. As Shelley Berman used to say, "A hotel is a place where you can spend an evening looking for a lamp switch." But, normally, after a minute or two, you will have fathomed the system – that is for arrival. You have yet to learn how to put the lights out when you eventually climb into bed.

Later will come your specialist lighting needs, such as reading in bed, applying makeup, or trying to find something in the closet. It is rare that the lighting designer has really considered all of these activities carefully. Designers often put more emphasis on how a light fixture looks, rather than how it performs. There often seems to be a gap in planning between the interior designer and the lighting consultant as to who is responsible for lighting systems in rooms. The answer, often is, that nobody really designs room lighting and it is often left to the construction project manager to improvise. This clearly is a mistake, since poor lighting in a room is a massive source of annoyance. Reading lights at bedside are frequently inadequate or extremely awkward to operate. They are likely to have been tried out by the design team in the day. The light source in closets is usually wrongly situated or too dim (often tested when there are no clothes in the closet) and it is rare to find the correct level of light for the application of makeup. All of these functions are essential for guests and are on their minimum list of expectancies.

Then, there is the question of light at night, when there is either too little of too much. Too little, perhaps because many of your hotel guests will need to find their way to the bathroom at night, and too much, because a room flooded with LED lights from television sets, minibars, alarm clocks and other electrical devices can shed so much light into a darkened room that one finishes up throwing a blanket over the television set. Worst of all, however, is the light from outside of the room. How many darkened hotel rooms are lit by neon signs outside on the building, or street lights or car headlights? If this is the case, management must make sure that an adequate blackout curtain is provided.

8. The noise

Most hotel rooms, sadly, are not very soundproof. Listening to lovemaking in the next room might be amusing for a while, but continuous noise from partying becomes annoying. Management must instruct staff to be prepared to deal with the problem of noisy, sometimes raucous, neighbours. A 'no noise' rule after nine o'clock can be effective, provided that staff are obliged to follow through with its implementation. Obviously, the problem starts with inadequate construction design specification, because it is difficult, almost impossible, to correct once the hotel is operational. The problem, therefore, needs to be managed, through communication to and cooperation from the guests. It should not be ignored.

It is also annoying to have to listen to the news or any show on the television operating in an adjacent room. This is something that can be controlled by limiting the upper levels of sound capability on television sets. What is more difficult to control is noisy partying guests. Clearly you want your hotel guests to have a good time, but not at the expense of others. Most partygoers don't seem to get this, so, once again a few house rules must be enforced. Failure to do so will lose you more revenue than that coming in from the one-time party crowd.

Street noise is another matter. Some of the noise (but not all) is unavoidable but its minimisation can be dealt with through better window fittings. Noisy staff activity, however, can be controlled. It is extremely annoying, when you are trying to sleep, to hear staff shouting at each other in the corridor, or outside at the loading bay. It is aggravating to hear the garbage truck at 6 am. especially when this is often something that could be rescheduled. This may be understandable and unavoidable in Manhattan, but in most cases, a little bit of planning and disciplining by management can eliminate the babble.

Ice machines can also make an annoying noise, obviously more so in rooms closest to them. It is essential that they are situated in areas that, although easy to access, are completely sound proofed. The machine should not deliver ice until the door is closed.

If you are unlucky enough to be allocated a room near to a bank of elevators you may get dinged to death. There is no reason why the arrival of an elevator at your floor should be announced by a bell or buzz, especially one that resonates down the hallway and under the bedroom doors. This is something that can be eliminated immediately.

Door slamming in the hallway is a tough, but very frequent problem, particularly when a convention party, who always seem to be lodged on your floor, come back to their rooms after some hard partying. "See you in the morning!" they bellow down the hallway at each other and then, one by one, proceed to slam their doors. Each slam seems to rattle your own room door. The designer who can come up with silent closing hotel room doors will deserve a medal.

9. The plug-ins

The entertainment equipment, primarily through the tele-vision set, has improved immensely. The operation of the TV, however, has become more complicated and there is nothing more annoying than the hand controller which is missing, won't work, or is too complicated for the average guest over fifty. Maintenance staff get more calls from frus-trated TV operators than for any other matter. Surely, the industry could come up with a handset that is restricted to 'on', 'off', 'channel change', and 'volume change'? That way, no previous guest or current one could mess it up.

Then, of course, there is the content – and the information in the room pertaining to it. If I had a dollar for every time I have consulted the in room TV guide for the number of the channel to find that it is different on the screen, I would be a rich man. Surely this is something that man-agement could check on from time to time? Then there is the choice of content. With so many channels available, one would have thought that it would be possible to satisfy all guests' needs, no matter, where they come from or what language they speak. It is very annoying to find, when you settle down to watch the TV in the comfort of your room, that it does not carry the channel you need nor have programmes in your language. Also, with the explosion of streaming channels that are now available, with universal appeal, it would surely be of great service to hotel guests to be able to tune in to the feature that they have been watching at home. There may be a cost involved, but the hotel that can meet all the requirements of its clientele regarding television content, will be scoring high marks regarding satisfaction.

Most of your guests will want to work or play on a tablet, laptop, or another electronic gadget. Don't make life hard for them. Don't annoy them by making the connection process difficult or expensive. Don't set it up so that they have to repeatedly re-sign in. Make sure that the recharging plugs are accessible. It is annoying to guests to have to scramble on their knees to find a plug or move the desk, or whatever. Then, make sure that there is an uncluttered space for people to work, comfortably.

Consider carefully if you really need a clock in the room; it takes up bedside table space and, sometimes, throws out unwanted light. It is possible, in a universe married to cell phones, that the uses for the clock, (i.e. time telling, alarm waking etc.) are now redundant. This decision may be driven by the nature of your clientele. I am an old fellow; I quite like a clock.

10. The telephone

So far, the cell phone has not eliminated the need for an in-room phone. That is a shame because, without doubt, the phone in a hotel bedroom, is the most frustrating and annoying piece of equipment in the whole hotel. Firstly, the bedside version of it is normally too bulky for the size of the bedside table, eliminating a place for the book or the glasses or teeth, or whatever. Second, the writing and numbers on the phone are normally so small or indistinct that they cannot be deciphered without one's glasses – or even with them. Then, there are infuriating buttons, which, when pressed, do not lead one to the required and advertised destination. 'Fast track service', normally gets picked up, after many rings, by the front desk clerk, who then has to call someone else to attend to your need. Likewise, when you press many other of the multiple buttons. Making outgoing telephone calls, i.e. getting an outside line, can be a work of art or just plain luck. Making an international call can be a nightmare of logistics and a horror story of expense. Basically, most in room telephones are not fit for purpose, especially those that purport to have two or more lines. The answer to all of this is KISS – Keep it simple stupid!

Hoteliers should resist the telephone equipment salesmen. In this day of cell phones, which almost everybody uses for their phone communications, the in-room hotel phone is primarily used (apart, perhaps for a few local calls) as an in-house instrument or for incoming calls and should be designed as such. It should give you instant connection to the hotel departments that you need, quickly. Its dialling system should be in large print, and its instructions should be simple, straightforward, and clear. The less buttons and the more legible they are, the less annoying the whole in-house communication system will be. Maybe we should revert to the *Downton Abbey* model of ringing bells?

11. The curtains.

Window treatments are a very important factor in hotel bedrooms, not only because they perform an essential function but also because they are possibly the predominant decorative feature in the room. Firstly, the curtains must be functional; i.e. they must be capable of blocking out the light. So often they don't; either the material is too thin or the light floods in around the edges. On top of this, hotel room curtains are often very difficult for pull. Either the mechanisms are inaccessible, fouled up or broken.

Sometimes the curtains are faux and the blackout is performed by a blind. Quite often these blinds leak light, so you must ensure that they fit tightly to the window frames. The mechanisms which allow you to control these blinds and curtains can also be annoying, since they frequently get jammed or knotted. A room check, be it by housekeeper or manager, should always include the functioning and effectiveness of the window treatments.

Sometimes curtains and blinds are controlled electronically. This can be frustrating if the controls are not clear. For those that play with electric train sets it is probably all too easy to open and close your drapes and windows with a handheld control. For old chaps, like me, it sometimes takes a while to master the technique and can be pretty annoying if I fail, and the curtains just won't close by old fashioned muscle.

12. Printed material

There is normally quite a lot of printed matter in a hotel bedroom, but there are not always all the things you need. It is quite nice to have glossy magazines with adverts of goods that you could only dream of buying, but it is more important to provide essential information about the hotel's facilities, location and operating hours. It is probably redundant to include the menus of all of the restaurants (a description will probably suffice) but the full room service menu and hours of operation should be included. Where appropriate, a history of the hotel, its owners, and its clientele can be very interesting for strangers. However, in the case of all printed matter, it is important that it is legible and that it is refreshed from time to time. For this reason, a directory design that is loose-leaf will enable you to make changes without reprinting the whole tome. It is annoying and unpleasant to be looking through a dogeared, stained copy of the hotel directory or one which a previous guest has used as a writing pad, but, alas, that is often the case. The same applies to other printed matter. 'Do not disturb' and 'Please make up the room' door hanging cards get a lot of use. Make sure they are regularly replaced or are made in such a way that they are not easily damaged or defaced.

Printed messages on your pillow are a nice idea, particularly those that offer a weather forecast for the next day. The lack of them is not a dissatisfier, but the fact that someone has bothered to issue them can certainly be a guest pleaser. Leaving a chocolate on the pillow, which became quite a trend, always seemed an odd goodnight gift, given that one had probably just brushed one's teeth.

Whatever print you decide to leave in the room, please check that it makes sense and that it is legible. Finally, leave a writing pad and pencil or pen near the phone; your guests will be less likely to scribble on your guest directory. Remember, your guest is more than likely unfamiliar with the area, so a well thought through guide can be most welcome. So can a local map.

"Why don't you hire a woman to design your bathrooms? The lighting and mirrors are so bad that you cannot put your make-up on without looking like Charlie Chaplin, and there is nowhere to put your washbags and other paraphernalia that ladies carry."

– DOLORES DELARGO, SILVER LAKE, LA

"I fell over and bruised my arm, whilst getting out of the bathtub. You should provide non slip mats and grab bars."

– LUCY SPRAWL, VENTNOR, NJ, USA

"Why do you provide such silly small pieces of soap? And why are they so tightly wrapped up that I have to wrestle with them?"

– MRS POLLY SUDLESS, TRURO, UK

"There is black mould in the shower. It is disgusting!"

– JANET GRIMES, NEWCASTLE, UK

"I could not work the shower. I felt such a fool, but I just couldn't figure it out. Turns out it was broken; your housekeeping should have noticed this!"

– MRS JANET TWIDDLE, ONTARIO

Chapter Three
The Bathroom

The word 'bathroom' is probably obsolete. The percentage of hotel room guests who actually take a bath is now very small, since most take showers. As a result of trying to please everybody, bathtubs are often still installed, so showers need to be taken in a bath, which, of course is not only cack-handed but also can be awkward and even dangerous. On the scale of hotel guest needs, the bathroom ranks, after the bed, as the most important facility that a hotel must provide. It is a great shame, therefore, that it is often given so little attention in the hotel design process. Much has been achieved in bathroom design over many years, yet bathroom design, facilities, maintenance, and operation can still rank high on the list of 'dissatisfiers'.

1. First impression

Your guest's first impression of the bathroom, as the accompanying receptionist offers the redundant words "and this is your bathroom," should be "Wow!" The bathroom should be a gleaming and sparkling, like a toothpaste advert. It should be so light and bright that you won't actually focus in what it contains or how it is laid out. The light should be bouncing off the shining tiles and mirrors. It should be warm and welcoming. Alas, this is not always the case. First impression can be of a dull little box with a flickering light filtering through a plastic ceiling shade, accompanied by the rattle of an ancient exhaust system. In these cases, guests immediately check to see if it contains everything that they will need, i.e. towels, plastic cups, etc. That is to say, they will start to look for things that are missing. When you are blown away, you will assume, often incorrectly, that the hotel manager will have thought of everything that you need.

2. Maxing out the space

Bathrooms are traditionally small spaces. Clearly, they have specific, time limited, usage and do not form part of the living space. They are wet rooms, which require hard surfaces, which are not conducive with 'comfortable' living. Keeping them small also keeps down construction costs. However, because of this, there is a school of design thought which considers it luxurious to offer grand bathrooms, both in size and style. The thinking is to provide the visitor with something sumptuous and spacious that they would not have in their own 'mundane' homes or lives. However, in most instances space and cost do not allow for spacious bathrooms in hotel rooms, so other innovative designs have been tried to give the feeling of more space.

Some designers have tried placing the bathtub in the actual bedroom. Pictorially this approach has a certain sex appeal, but practically, it is unworkable for double occupancy and can be annoying to both occupants. Other approaches have been to open up the wet bathroom area to the bedroom with glass walls or folding panels. This has the effect of making the overall room look bigger by removing one of the internal walls, but, again, most double occupancy inhabitants keep the folding doors closed for privacy, particularly when the WC is located in the bathroom.

It is more normal (and practical) to revert to the separate bathroom, where ablutions can be apart from the soft furnishings of the living and sleeping areas. In these cases, the obvious way to free up space is to remove the tub and enhance the shower and vanity space. But, make sure this extra space is used wisely. A source of constant annoyance in hotel bathrooms is the lack of shelf space to accommodate guest's washbags, make up bags etc. particularly if the room is occupied by two or more people. There is normally no reason for this since, in most cases, the space below the vanity is not often well utilised.

The same thing applies to the vanity top, whether there are one or two sinks. Often, there is not enough space for guests to even leave their toothbrushes, let alone their toothpaste, their shaving cream, their razor, their dental floss, their aspirin, their deodorant – and that is just for the men! Management must think through this valuable space carefully; it is highly sought after!

3. The shower and tub

Showers have come a long way since the ones where you held a sprinkler in your hand whilst sitting in the bath. However, whether they are above the bathtub or in a shower cubicle, they tend to have their own special characteristics, some of which can be rather annoying. The first challenge is normally to fathom out how to turn the wretched thing on without spraying yourself, or the bathroom, with cold or scalding water. That is normally due to the fact the controls can be often unnecessarily complicated and frequently situated in the wrong place. What is wrong with one lever that changes the water flow from cold to hot as you move it and is sited away from the gushing stream? Shower controls that require an engineering degree to fathom out how they work serve no other purpose than to annoy the guest. Then, there is the water temperature. One of the most aggravating things to a guest in a hotel is its inability to supply hot water. Hot water is something that every guest expects to be able to get. On the other hand, water that is too hot can be dangerous. Nor should the temperature of the water in one shower fluctuate when the person in the adjacent room flushes their toilet.

Showering in a hotel bathtub can also be an adventure, sometimes a difficult one. You will do more than annoy your guests if they slip in the tub; you will be taking them to the hospital; so, make sure that there is a nonslip mat available and a grab handle to boot.

Then there is the view from the tub. Try sitting in the tub and casting your eye around the bathroom. This is not a view a Manager, or Housekeeper, will get from a walk-in room inspection. It may well be that from the tub you can see all of the pipework that feeds the vanity bowls. This view is sometimes a mess, but it is a mess that all bathtub bathing guests will see.

4. The towels

Towels are also items that a hotel guest will reasonably expect to be provided with. It is, therefore, annoying to find that a king or queen bedded room has often only been supplied with one set of towels. If a hotel has a high single occupancy in its king/queen bedded rooms, it is possible that the practice has been to supply one set of towelling. If this is the policy of the hotel, then that policy must extend to alerting the front desk, that this is really a single, not double room. It is annoying having to call housekeeping when you are about to shower because of a lack of linen. The supply of sufficient and adequate towels is something that every guest expects; without that they will be dissatisfied. However, if the towel supply is more than adequate and if the towels are super soft and luxuriously thick, the hotel will have exceeded expectations and the guest will be happy. Even better if the towel rail has heated the towels to a nice toasty state. Old, hard towels, threadbare towels, undersized towels, are all big dissatisfiers, as is the absence, quite frequently, of face cloths.

And pay attention to where the towels are hung or stored in the bathroom. Your guest should not need to be a gymnast to reach them. And, if you do offer a turn down service, don't take away the used towels and facecloths without replacing them; people do shower late.

5. The amenities

Bathrobes are always welcome. They can give a luxurious 'feel' even in a cheap hotel. But make sure that they are large enough to fit most of your clientele because it is rather deflating for them to find they won't. Hairdryers are important, and shoehorns are useful. However, none of these things are essential; they are just showing that management is going the extra mile.

On the other hand, the bathroom amenities are essential, including bars of soap. These should be large enough for ease of handling and not annoyingly wrapped so that they are difficult to open. Other amenities, including shampoo, conditioner and shower gel may be from a luxury brand, but if the writing on the container is too small to read, then a 'satisfier' is turned immediately into an annoyance. Remember, hotel guests to not wear their spectacles in the shower, so how are the supposed to read labels that are as small as newsprint?

6. The john or WC

The toilet seat holds a very special place in a hotel room. It is something every guest will use – and needs. So why not pay some attention to it? It should not be an afterthought or something just dumped there by the plumber. First of all, it should be comfortable – or at least as comfortable as a hard surface on human skin can be. It must never look worn or discoloured. Most guests seem to think it should be white, presumably because it looks cleaner. It must not wobble about and it must be thoroughly clean, including the hinges and fittings. From the guests' perch the view must be acceptable and perhaps even enlivened by artwork. The toilet tissue must be within easy reach. It is rather annoying, to say the least, to have to grope for the necessary, when it has been awkwardly placed. This sounds rather basic but, quite frequently, guests find that they need long and/or flexible arms to reach the loo roll. There should also be a spare roll within easy reach and it is a false economy (and annoying to the guest) to use paper that is too thin or too narrow; they will just use more! If the water closet is enclosed in its own space, rather than in the bathroom proper, then it must be properly ventilated, but such ventilation should not back onto the guest corridor. Finally, there must be a workable lock on the door. You would think that all of this would be bog standard, but there are hotel loos and hotel loos.

7. Lighting

If lighting is important anywhere in a hotel, it is in the bathroom. It is here that men shave and ladies apply makeup. Neither of these are easy without fit for purpose lighting and appropriate mirrors. According to Mrs Venison, hotels almost always get this wrong. The mirror is fixed too high or too low, and, if it happens to be in the right place, there often is no light source near it, or only from one side. Some hotels make a feeble attempt to solve this problem by furnishing the room with a small makeup mirror on the desk in the bedroom. This invariably is useless, due to inappropriate lighting. This is a problem that can be easily solved and should be addressed in the critique of a mock up room before construction, although it can be retrofitted at little expense.

Bathroom lighting needs to be bright. However, at night, a bright light shining out into the bedroom can disturb the sleep of the second person in the room. Often, too, the switching on of the bathroom light can activate a fan, often with its collateral whirring or rattling noise, which will certainly wake up your partner if the light didn't. To alleviate this, the installation of a low-level night light in the bathroom works well.

Finally, whilst in the electrical section of the bathroom, pay attention to the frequency, range, and location of the electrical sockets. They need to be plentiful enough for joint use of electric razor, electric toothbrush and, maybe, the hairdryer. One universal plug situated out of reach at the end of a fluorescent tube is not good enough.

"I could have bought a new shirt for the price they charged to wash one."

– JAMES SMART, WESTMINSTER

"It was Sunday evening and the hotel restaurant was closed, so we had to order on room service. The whole thing was shambolic. First, it took forty minutes for our food to arrive and then, when it did, it was all squashed onto one tray so the fries had fallen off their dish and the sauce from my pasta had got mixed up with my wife's salad. There was no proper table to eat from, only a low coffee table and only one chair in the room. On top of that, they charged us extra for using room service, when there was nowhere else to go. We will not stay here again."

– (NAME WITHHELD, SARASOTA, FLORIDA)

"I sent my laundry and ticked off all the little boxes on the form. When it came back each handkerchief was individually wrapped in plastic, as were all my underpants. There is a note in the bathroom to request that one reuses the towels to save the ecology, but you drown me with plastic!"

– BASIL GREEN, LIMOGES, FRANCE

"After the maid's so-called turn down service, I had no facecloths, and only one towel; also, the robe was missing. Unfortunately, my used beer glass and empty bottle were still there. Very sloppy!"

– REGINALD TIDY, SHEPPERTON, UK

Chapter Four
Services to the Room

All bedrooms in hotels need servicing, even in no-service hotels. Even in the most basic establishment there will be a need for maid service and, from time to time, maintenance. In full-service hotels, of course, the complete range of services is required. These services are, by their nature, quite difficult to supervise or check quality control. Most of them take place in the hideaway spaces of hotel bedrooms, making oversight difficult. The concept of supervision, i.e. looking over something or someone to see if they are doing it right, cannot apply, since you can't have any 'vision' of what is going on. As a Manager, you are entirely reliant on either spot checking, regular inspection, or guest feedback. It is therefore important that you train and trust, but you cannot assume that everything is going right.

1. Room service

Not nearly enough attention is paid by Management to the finer points of food and beverage room service, from the menu selection, the equipment, and the delivery. This really is a case of 'the devil is in the detail'. There is no point in offering menu items that do not lend themselves to fitting

on a tray or will spoil due to either travel time or distur-
bance. Items offered should lend themselves to packaging
and presentation. Trays should be designed to accommodate the selected menu. It is pretty annoying to receive a
room service delivery where the tray is so overcrowded that
the chips are balanced on top of the salad, or the sauces have
overflowed onto the tray cloth.

Food and beverage delivery equipment should be carefully
considered. The industry norms are trolleys with heated
cabinets or simple trays. The trolleys with their flip-up
table flaps rarely fit into the hotel room, at least with any
space around them for two chairs, even if the room actually
has two chairs, which it probably doesn't (and, even if it
did, they would be of the wrong height!). The trays, whilst
normally adequate for a lone diner, are never large enough
to accommodate two meals, but, come what may, the staff
attempt to squeeze on both.

Ordering the food and drink can also be a mission. Printed
room service menus are often too specific or limited for
most guest's tastes, with the result that the order taker has
to grasp with add on orders which they often do not understand. The staff position of room service order taker is a very
important one and should not be delegated to the lowest
level worker, especially if the language of the hotel is not
their first one, which is likely to be the case. Room service
is one of the flash points of interaction between guest and
staff; there are so many opportunities to get things wrong.
(See Shelley Berman's description in Appendix 2.)

Management's attention to room service is not often prioritised above that of the restaurant. That is a mistake,
because, in many cases, the use of room service is the only

live service requirement of a guest, particularly singles or travelling businessmen, who simply want to chill out in their room at the end of a busy day. Room service is one of the fault lines between hotel and guest, where things can go badly wrong or points can be scored.

Trolleys are often not properly wiped down between uses, trays are left outside hotel doors for too long, the time from order to delivery is often excessive, the quality and temperature of the food delivered is often not up to standard, and to top it all, there is normally a delivery charge levied. How annoying is that? Most guests are irked to be asked to pay extra for their chips when they are not even taking up a restaurant seat, but slumming it in their pyjamas?

Attention to room service standards is often low priority for hotel managers. The preparation area for room service trays and trolleys is often an afterthought in the planning and design process and it is shunted into a corner or hallway where it is difficult to supervise. That is a mistake; make the streamlining of your room service as important as polishing the stars on your restaurant. It is a great opportunity for you and your hotel to shine.

2. Maid service

Maid service is obviously the most commonly used service of all hotel services. It is one of the few services provided in a hotel that the guest does not have to request. It also comes included in the price. It can, however, be taken for granted by hotel managers, who are fooled into thinking it is one of the simplest services to offer and, therefore, what possibly could go wrong? Lots of things! Just because housekeeping is often staffed by low paid immigrants at the bottom of the employment ladder and is regarded as unskilled labour, that does not mean that the service provided by hotel maids is unimportant. Actually, it is the single most important service offered by a hotel and your maids should be made aware that it is viewed as such. Making sure that your maids are doing an excellent job and telling them so is important.

Until a room is ready for occupancy it cannot be rented. Until the guest has departed from the room, it obviously cannot be readied for the next guest. This sets up a potential conflict between the room maid and the room clerk, but the room maid holds the power. The receptionist cannot allocate the room to a waiting guest until the housekeeping supervisor has checked that the maid has done her work. This interface between one department of a hotel and another is one of several that have the potential to cause a problem. Who loses out? The guest! It is always an interesting dilemma when a perceived 'junior' member of staff holds some sway over one more 'senior'. It is the same when a 'junior' waiter goes into the kitchen to give the 'senior' cook an 'order'. If the job titles get in the way, the guest/diner suffers.

In a busy hotel it is essential that rooms of departing guests are prioritised for cleaning before resident guests, and it is essential that they are done so in an order that works best for the front desk. So here is another potential conflict, wherein one department of the hotel is telling another department how to do their job. It is management's job to build cooperation, and downplay competitiveness and competition.

Maids are important spokes in the wheel of the hotel; they must be treated so by management and understand the importance of their role. But they must be trained properly and supervised to check that their performance is up to standard, which means that clear standards must be set, explained and maintained. First is the maid's (and housemen's) appearance. The work is quite physical, so the uniform must not only be attractive but also practical to account for, sometimes, dirty work, lifting, carrying, bending and so on. The maid must look tidy and so should the maid's cart or basket. Nothing looks worse from the guest's point of view than a traffic jam of untidy maids' carts in a hallway. The cart must always look well organised. Unorganised carts equal waste and, therefore, cost. Your maids must appreciate that guest's habits differ. Some will want to sleep late, some may have just arrived on an over-night flight, some might be on a different time zone, etc. Maids who shout to each other down the long and sound reverberating hallways of a hotel are not helpful.

Then, there is the actual in-room work of the maid. Most important, of course, is the making of the bed. This should be done in a uniform manner. Setting this standard and ensuring that all maids are conversant with it is one of man-agement's most important tasks. It should not be beneath the dignity of a hotel manager to show someone how to make a bed. I would venture to suggest that most hotel managers have never actually physically set up this stan-dard. That done, it is certainly necessary to maintain the standard by frequent inspection, of every bedroom, every day, by the floor supervisor, frequently by the housekeeper, and on a random basis each week by the hotel manager. Standards set without quality checks will not work.

For hotels that offer a turn down service, management should consider what it is attempting to achieve, and then check that it is doing so. Through cost cutting pressure, many turn down services have degenerated into a quick glance around the room by a maid with too many rooms to handle. It is annoying, as a guest, to go back to your hotel room after the so-called turn down has taken place to find that your used beer glass is still on the table or the facecloths you used in the morning have been whipped away and not replenished. It is also irritating to be interrupted for 'turn down' just as you are dressing to go out to dinner. Interruptions at the wrong time are like receiving sales phone calls just as you are sitting down to dinner. The turn down process was originally designed to replenish and refresh the room and bathroom AFTER it has been used during the day, in order to make sure that the room is properly equipped for the evening and the next morning. It is pretty pointless doing this at 2 pm, just because the maid's shift finishes at 3 pm. This is the cart leading the horse and the guest does not want to return to his room after lunch to find the drapes have been drawn and Beethoven is on the music box.

Finally, remember that the contact between maid and guest is an important one. It is another opportunity for the guest to be made to feel that she is in a home away from home. Encourage your maids to be friendly to your guests, encourage them to ask if anything extra is needed, and encourage them to make the guest feel that they are the guest's personal maid. Try not to rotate the maids so that they are always moving floors; let them own their territory and their special guests. Do not fall into the trap of 'contract' cleaners; they will do nothing to make your guests feel loved. For further information re the relationship between hotel guest and maid, please see Appendix 3 at the end of this book.

3. Maintenance service

The maintenance man is the stepchild of the family. Maintenance is often not regarded by hotel management as a guest service at all. How wrong is that? You can be pretty certain that most hotel guests have at some time needed the services of 'maintenance'. Partly, because of their perceived role as not being in the front line of service, maintenance staff are often treated that way by management and not as involved in discussions around 'service' that they might be. Often scant attention is given to their uniforms or to their training in guest relations. Make no mistake, however, the maintenance men are very much part of the service team, even if they are kept at bay. It is almost as if management think that maintenance staff will be incapable of speaking to guests. If you check out the push buttons on the in-room phone you will rarely see 'maintenance', because you are rarely put, as a guest, into direct contact with them. Your phone call to ask about the a/c controls or the TV set will normally be routed through a housekeeper or desk clerk, who will probably tell you that they "will pass on the message to maintenance." Next you will get a call or visit from maintenance to find out what the problem is, even though you have explained it to the clerk. Or, as frequently happens, the first responder, who is normally technically incompetent, will come to your room with the good intention of fixing the problem, only to find that he or she can't (otherwise you probably would have been able to) and then announces that he or she will 'call maintenance'.

The role of the maintenance department in relation to the guest could do with a rethink. Maintenance issues are high up the list of guest 'dissatisfiers'. Getting the maintenance right will not have your hotel guests going home raving about the hotel, but it will prevent them from going home ranting.

Elevate your maintenance men to be seen by themselves and the rest of the staff as a vital part of the service team, not just in regard to the back of the house, but also in relation to the guests. Make sure that your maintenance staff are properly trained in regard to guest contact. There can be a tendency for them to give the impression that your non-techy guests are dummies. Remember, the guest is always right, even if he can't recognise the 'on' button.

4. Laundry service

Getting your laundry done can be full of surprises. A laundry list can normally be found somewhere in the room, even if you have to search a bit. To facilitate this service guests are normally asked to tick off items to be laundered, pressed, or cleaned on the list, together with any special instructions. In many hotels the prices are so high that you could practically buy new items for the cost of laundering the old ones. Nevertheless, if you are particularly fond of the things you have been wearing, you will probably use the hotel laundry service or, as provided in some hotels, you will do the work yourself at a guest laundry room situated somewhere in the bowels of the hotel.

If you are brave enough to risk the hotel laundry service and rich enough to pay for it, you will need to fill in the options on the checklist. When do you want it back by, how much starch do you need, and would you like certain items on hangers or folded? For some reason laundry service can be 50% to 100% more expensive if you want your shirts back today, as opposed to tomorrow – as if a few hours make much difference to the costs. That I find mildly annoying (gouging!), but it is more so when, upon the return of the laundry you find that nobody has read (maybe, could read) the instructions. Time and again, having asked for my shirts to be folded, they come back on hangers, which is just what I don't want when I come to repack my case!

Other annoying things about the laundry service is the propensity to wrap and double wrap one's returning clothes in plastic and tissue paper. On the one hand there is a sign in the bathroom asking you to reuse your towels in the interest of stopping global warming when, on the other, you are being showered with plastic bags. Then, there is the laundry bag itself. Either too small, too flimsy, or impossible to tie. And yes, you are right: inevitably, it will be plastic!

The condition of men's shoes used to be important, but the art of shoe shining seems to be dying. Partly, perhaps, because shoes have become more and more casual, and partly because there has been a more general move to casual attire across the world. Nevertheless, in some hotels, male guests do need to shine their shoes, so the provision of such a service should be reviewed by management. On the whole this service has ceased to be offered, but it is not difficult to organise (night staff often have time to spare), so why not tack it onto your laundry list? If this is not practical, the provision of a shoe shine kiosk, somewhere near your front door could be a winner and may not cost the hotel a dime.

"Why is it that the hotel shop never has the things you want? You would have thought that toothpaste would be a no- brainer!"

– GEORGE CREST, WINNIPEG, CANADA

"The banquet was nice – but I couldn't hear what anyone else at my table said. The band was so loud. I also couldn't see across the table because the view was obscured by a huge bowl of flowers; although they were lovely flowers. Why don't the people who organise these things think about how it works?"

– MRS LILLIAN PLEASANT, BOSTON, MASS

"The hotel was quite alright, but the breakfast was always shambolic. I felt that I had to line up for everything like I was in the army. First, to get into the room, then to get to the toaster, then to get some coffee. This was ridiculous."

– IVOR CONTINENTAL, NASHVILLE

"The hotel had this fantastic pool; it was huge. I've never seen such a beautiful pool. But, guess what? You could never find anywhere to sit or sunbathe. The Germans had all been down at about five in the morning and grabbed all of the loungers. Somebody should have done something to control that. It wasn't fair and it rather spoiled my holiday."

– DIANA PALEFACE, SOUTH MIMMS

"I wanted the starter from the table d'hôte menu but the main from the a la carte. I told the waiter that I was willing to pay extra. He said that it was not possible. I told him that, of course it was possible and couldn't he just bend the rules to accommodate me? He refused to do it. I was quite cross."

– MADAME BRIGITTE MARTIN, VERSAILLES, FRANCE.

Chapter Five
The Lobby and Other Public Areas

The hotel lobby is your showpiece; this is the area that has maximum impact on your guest. It is your very own 'front room' and it should be on its best behaviour at all time. Just as you might spruce up the cushions on the couch in your parlour when guests are due, you need to do this, continuously, in the hotel 'parlour'. This is the room where the big bucks have been spent on décor. This is the hotel's chance to impress. This is where people go to see people and to be seen. The human race is gregarious. Being 'locked away' in a hotel room is not natural. There are, of course, times when the room becomes a haven but, after a while, a haven can feel more like a prison. The public areas of the hotel offer contact with the rest of the human race. The lobby is the village centre, the green, the market place. This is particularly important in resort hotels, where the length of stay is extended. It is vital for management to think of the lobby in this way and to make sure that it is really fulfilling its function.

But remember, just a little way from this centrepiece are adjacent areas where the public and hotel guests might also roam. The toilets, the hallways to the banqueting rooms, the entrance to the hotel's administration and so on. These adjuncts to your hotel showpiece are as important as your downstairs 'loo' at home.

So, as Manager of the hotel, take time out to sit quietly in your lobby and watch. Arrange to meet people in the lobby rather than in your office. Lose yourself for half an hour in a corner and observe. Staying in one spot for ten minutes or so can be far more rewarding than merely walking through. Is your lobby functioning as it should – or could?

1. The design

The lobby design will differ dependent upon the nature of the hotel (business or resort) and, of course, its size. It is very annoying for arriving guests, having possibly travelled a long and tiring way, to have to stand in line to check-in. Likewise, it is annoying to have to line up to pay one's bill at the end of the stay. With the marvels of electronic charging, the latter is absolutely unnecessary. The sight of roped off lines to cope with arrivals and departures is reminiscent of sheep shearing, not hospitality.

The two main aspects of lobby design are aesthetic and functionality. Both are important. If the basic functions of check-in and check-out are not handled well, naturally there will be much dissatisfaction. That is not to say that people will be satisfied if these run smoothly, because they expect them to. Functionality is dealing with the expected; aesthetics is dealing with blowing away the customer. Lobby architecture and décor are a hotelier's biggest opportunity to create a wow factor on a scale not possible in a domestic setting.

The design must allow for comfortable check-in and swift check-out, so the size of the desks or counters must be able to cope with a crowd. For large group check- ins a special area should be available, so as not to interfere with the other guests. The distribution of keys and information to groups should be pre-planned with the cooperation of group leaders.

The design must also allow for plenty of comfortable seating. This will be required for guests awaiting the availability of rooms, guests waiting for transportation, guests meeting visitors, business tête-à-têtes, non-residents as a meeting place, and hotel guests who simply want to get out or their rooms. If space permits the lobby should have interesting things for guests to read or do.

If the décor can highlight things of local interest it is often appreciated. Hotel lobbies that offer food and beverage service are most popular for guests and revenue producing, so access (and visual access) to services is essential.

So, what can annoy guests about your lobby? Not enough seats. Lobby doors that allow a gale to rush through the room as they frequently open and close.

Piped music that drives you mad. Messy posters and advertisements stuck on walls, irrespective of their negative impact on the planned décor. Untidy travel and tour desks. Excessively noisy surfaces. Plastic flowers.

2. The concierge

The importance of the concierge cannot be overstated. He or she is the 'go to' person in the hotel. A good concierge should be like local Wikipedia. They should be able to answer almost any question and provide any information required from a guest, as it relates to the vicinity of the hotel. They are also a human link between guest and staff, particularly if hotel management is conspicuous by its absence. However, something strange can happen to a man or woman when they don the badge of the golden keys. They can be prone to a certain pomposity. They can also practice selective attention to the guests. The concierge, who clearly is not interested in explaining to a tourist where the local bus stops, because he or she is too busy cosying up to the guest that arrived in the 'Roller', is not a good ambassador for your hotel. Nor is the concierge who only recommends establishments from which they have negotiated a kickback.

A good concierge will entertain all comers, be they rich or poor, individual or group member, because they are all guests of their employer, the hotel. A good concierge will have a plentiful supply of local maps and a good knowledge of tourist and cultural attractions, as well as restaurants, clubs, theatres and other places of entertainment or interest. Whereas 'googling' can be of great help to your concierge, one who relies on this to answer every question can be irritating because guests are looking for a personal recommendation, not something canned.

3. The hotel shop

A good hotel shop can be a lifesaver for travelling guests. Whether it is to replenish something in their washbags, or to buy a last-minute souvenir to take home to the kids, a properly stocked shop can be very useful.

If your hotel incorporates a shop, or shops, however small, the chances are that it is leased from you and operated by an independent. This arrangement is of no interest to your guest, so any behaviour exhibited by the shop salesperson will be seen as behaviour of a member of your staff, not your lessee. It so often happens that the hotel shop does not carry the items that the hotel guest is looking for, or is closed when required. Put yourself in the shoes of your guest to think through what items are most likely to be required by a traveller, from toothpaste to the *New York Times*, and insist that your shopkeeper carries these items at all times. Make sure, also, that the shop has a stock of items that are locally produced or are in some way associated with the area. And, insist that the shop is open at hours that coincide with the majority of hotel guests' presence rather than the whims of the lessee. Also, keep an eye on the prices. There is a tendency for hotel shops to charge considerably more than high street stores since they offer convenience to a captive market. This is to be expected up to a point. Make sure that your guests are not being gouged in your hotel shop because it will reflect badly on you. Finally, pay attention to the appearance of the shop and its displays. There is little point in paying an interior designer if an untidy shopkeeper is going to mess up the plan.

4. The banquet rooms

Most hotels will have some form of meeting facility or private dining rooms. These will often comprise of reception rooms and larger rooms, which can often be subdivided. Many hotels will have separate entrances, other than the main lobby, for guests arriving for a function or meeting. These facilities can be dressed up to look quite spectacular for functions, which is how most people will see them. However, there is nothing worse than the sight of a function room after the function, with tables and chairs in disarray, sliding doors open, service doors ajar, unfinished flip charts or old bouquets or whatever. Remember, some of your hotel guests may be on the prowl, and if your function facilities adjoin other public areas of the hotel, then there is a reasonable chance that some of your hotel guests will chance upon them. Function rooms that are not in use should either be locked off from public (hotel guest) access or left in a state of readiness and tidiness that will impress.

This also applies to the banqueting restrooms, which, if available to hotel guests, will certainly get used.

In regards to the operation of the function rooms there are also practices which are aggravating. Take the matter of table seating plans, which are normally displayed on boards at the entrance to the banquet hall. These should always be displayed alphabetically, not, as they are in most cases, by table number. They should also be well lit and there should be sufficient plans for all guests to find out where they are seated quickly and comfortably. And the print should be large enough for even old men to read. If you do not follow these simple rules you will find a crush of irritated attendees, many with poor eyesight, scanning every table on the diagram until they find their name. Not a great start to the evening!

Banquet table sizes should be limited to eight persons. Above that any meaningful conversation is impossible, except the person on either side of you, which means that they cannot be in conversation with the person next to them. And don't get greedy by trying to squeeze too many tables into the available space, even if you are under pressure from your client. It is very annoying to be seated at a gala dinner to be constantly pushed in the back by other attendees trying to circulate. Furthermore, do not allow your florist to produce centrepieces, however lovely, that prevent guests seeing diners on the other side of the table. A banquet is supposed to be a social occasion. If you keep placing barriers to communication between people it defeats the object. Live entertainers need to be managed, just as other staff. They have a tendency to get louder and louder, forgetting that they are there to entertain you, not drown you. Similarly, they have a habit of taking a break, just as the party is getting going. If bands must have breaks, they should be properly managed and not interrupt the momentum.

Pay particular attention to the arrival process at any function of meeting taking place. If you are serving finger snacks make sure they are just that – capable of being held easily from serving dish to mouth. Also, don't leave people stranded with an empty wine glass because there is no way to dispose of it. Then, when announcements are made to proceed to the main room, make sure that the entrances are wide enough to avoid a bottle neck. People who have taken the trouble to dress up for an event do not want to be crushed as they try to get to it.

The lighting of function rooms is also extremely important. Multipurpose function rooms will need to be equipped with a range of lights to accommodate all needs, from business meetings to romantic evenings. Too much light or too little light can ruin an atmosphere.

Guests leaving a function can often be quite noisy, especially if the wine and spirits have been flowing freely. Be aware that this can be a huge problem for your in-house guests, especially if the function is emptying out late at night. It is possible that many of the banquet attendees will not be staying in the hotel, so there could be much banging of car doors and loud farewells outside the hotel, which might also be outside the hotel bedrooms. For those attendees who are resident, you can be sure that they will start shouting 'goodnights' to each other in the hallways before they slam their bedroom doors. Management must do whatever they can to mitigate this with signs and personnel to politely remind banquet guests that there are people sleeping nearby. Some late-night noise, however, is under the control of management. Rooftop nightclubs or discos whose music reverberates through the concrete structure of the buildings need to be thought about carefully, especially during the design phase of a hotel. It is not a good idea to operate a disco a few feet above the most prestigious suites in a hotel. The penthouses are often at the top because the view is the best. Discos don't need a view. In fact, most people like to go down to a club, not up.

5. The breakfast room

Breakfast is the most important meal of the day in most hotels, particularly business hotels, simply because breakfast is the only meal that you can be pretty sure most of your clientele will take. It is, therefore, the meal to which management should pay great attention. Breakfast time is also the best opportunity for a hotel manager to meet his guests, because almost all of the diners will be staying in the hotel. Breakfast is also, notoriously, the most difficult meal to cater. "I would like my egg three and a half minutes." "I would like my toast crisp, but not too crisp." "I would like orange, not cherry jam." "I need unsweetened almond milk, not cow's milk" and so on. There are just so many variables to cater for and it is served when people are in a hurry to get on with their day. The solution to the problem has been the breakfast buffet, but, that said, there are buffets and there are buffets!

What's wrong with the average hotel breakfast buffet? First, the equipment. Everybody knows that breakfast is a daily ritual, so why is it that it is often served up on makeshift, temporary equipment? You've all seen it. Trestle tables covered, often unevenly, with tablecloths, holding a variety of bain-maries, trays and miscellaneous kitchen equipment. If there is any 'live' cooking it is often on a makeshift griddle. Sometimes these Heath Robinson setups are in the restaurant, and sometimes in a hallway leading to the restaurant. Almost always they are unsatisfactory – and unnecessary. It is understandable that the provision of a proper range or permanent equipment in a dining room will, to some extent define the use of the room for lunch and dinner, but one has to say, what is more important? The provision of a proper breakfast facility for the benefit of all of your hotel guests or the décor for the dinner trade, which may not include a great number of your residents?

There is, of course, a school of thought, often articulated by management of luxury hotels, that it is wrong to expect guests to help themselves from a buffet; that this would never be done in *Downton Abbey*. However, due to the range of possibilities in a breakfast menu and the nuances of individual taste within that range, it does seem sensible to allow guests to help themselves, provided, of course, that the full range of possibilities is catered for on the buffet and provided that the items thereon are always fresh or freshly cooked.

The best way to achieve this goal is to incorporate a cooking station or stations within the buffet so that certain items, particularly eggs, can be cooked to order in front of the customer. This has the added advantage of creating a natural contact point between the staff and the customer. The more opportunity your guests have to interact with the staff, the more at home they will feel.

That said, there are many things on hotel breakfast buffets that are annoying. Let's start with those plastic drums full of cereal. You can tell that the contents are not fresh when the contents stick together and won't fall easily out onto your waiting bowl. That is, if you can find a bowl. Then there is the 'fresh' orange juice, which isn't. Then, can you find the no-fat milk or unsweetened almond milk? Probably not. Of course, you are going to get your fingers greasy, unwrapping solidly frozen (or runny) mini packs of butter. And don't search too long for marmalade because they have every other fruit preserve that you can think of, except the one you want. Then, why is it that the bowls of fruit are all from a tin, when you know that the greengrocers down the road is overflowing with fresh fruit? And, why are there no plates left on the pile? And, why does the scrambled egg look like a stodgy pie? And why is the spoon for the tomatoes in the bain-marie with the sausages, which are now cold? And, why are the glasses provided for the so-called fruit juices so small – it only means that you have to take two? And, what was in those dishes that are now empty? And why is there a traffic jam at the toaster and the coffee machine? How many more annoying things can you think of? Well, there is always the music.

It need not be that bad. It really is only a matter of organisation and management. All the more reason for the Hotel Manager to spend a good deal of time in the breakfast room, with his eyes and ears open. So, as a manager, when you arrive at work, before you head for the hideaway of your office, go to the breakfast room. This is the best chance you will have all day of meeting your guests. Not only will you receive valuable feedback about the performance of your hotel (far better that a guest questionnaire or après visit computer survey), whilst you still have the opportunity to do something about it while your complaining guests are still in house. You will also have the chance to look objectively at your buffet.

The best breakfast buffets are the ones that combine some cooking in front of the guest, an exceptional range of self-serve items, constant replenishment of, not only, food and beverage, but also serving equipment.

6. The restaurant

You will need to decide what your restaurant is for, or, to be more precise, for whom is it catering? Your thinking will, in the main, be driven by the needs of your hotel room guests, and these, of course, will be different according to the style and location of your property. The dining needs of resort guests may be completely different from those of a city hotel or a roadside motel. In all cases, however, the primary decision as to what type of restaurant is required revolves around your bedroom occupants, not in appealing to the outside world, unless you are in a position to satisfy both markets, possibly with multiple dining rooms.

In a resort, you are not simply satisfying the hunger of your guests; you are entertaining them and you are providing them with a social platform to interact with each other, to see each other and to be seen by each other. I am always reminded of the occasion when, in accompanying an advertising friend of mine to a famous (and hard to get in to) restaurant in New York, and, on being ushered to a prime table in the centre of the room, my commenting that "This is a nice table. You can see everyone from here." My friend's response was, "No, everybody can see you from here!" Dining in a resort is a social event, even before it is a gastronomic one. Not to say that the food and service shouldn't be good, but it is the social ambiance that makes the evening, and even the vacation. I can remember staying at a very exclusive island resort with my wife, where management twigged the fact that it was our wedding anniversary. As a result, they kindly opened the à la carte restaurant, especially for us and produced a special menu. It would be wrong to say that we did not have a beautiful meal but we were alone, and although we had much to reminisce about, after the meal we gravitated to the poolside bar, where all of the rest of the guests had been dining, because there was absolutely no atmosphere where we were.

Resort hotel restaurants must also figure out how to ring the changes in the menu and to create surprises because most of their guests will be staying for a least a week and, sometimes much longer. The food offerings must never become 'stale'. If buffets are used, they must feature different stations on different evenings and have a range large enough to please all comers. If buffets are used, they must be constantly replenished and the content should be changed from evening to evening. Ideally there should be no such thing as a dead buffet. The best buffets are those that are manned by the chefs, who can then interact with the guests and attend to their specific needs.

What is it that annoys resort guests in the dining room? Firstly, the scrum. The inevitable crowd that mill around certain sections of a buffet. Since this happens evening after evening in many resorts, it would not seem to be beyond the ability of man to ascertain the reason for the scrum and resolve it. Then there is the repetitiveness. To serve the same menu on the same crockery every day of a guest's stay is awful. Can you imagine, at home, having the same meal for seven evenings in a row? Then there is the rigidity of the separation of the table d'hôte from the à la carte. We have all experienced the battle with the waiter when you decide that you would like one dish that is featured on the menu of the day and another on the à la carte', even after making it clear that you are willing to pay the extra. "It is not possible," the waiter will exclaim, as if he is a throwback from communist Europe. "Why is it not possible?" you feebly ask, only to be told again, "It is just not possible." Well, of course, we all know that anything is possible – so this attitude and behaviour is really annoying.

Then there is the table plan. It seems that all restaurants have 'good' tables and 'bad' ones. But why? The design goal in a restaurant should be to make every table a good one, and, space permitting, this is possible. But, on the assumption that you do not have the perfect restaurant lay out, you must find a way to make sure that no one guest (or couple) is lumbered with the worst table, evening after evening. One way to do this is to 'move' the restaurant. One night could be romantic poolside dining, another a beach barbecue, another a banquet in the dining room with a long table as if it were for a State visit at Windsor Castle and so on.

City hotel dining rooms probably do not need to entertain so much as to satisfy guests' hunger. That said, they can always be entertaining and sustaining. Above all, they must serve the needs of your hotel guests. It is very annoying indeed to be told, as a hotel guest, that the restaurant if 'full', or to be greeted at the door with "Have you made a reservation?" with the implied threat, and possibly fact, that without a reservation there will be no room for you. It is irritating to find that 'your' restaurant has been taken over by a gang of people who aren't even staying in the hotel. Alternative suggestions from the hostess that you can eat in the bar or on room service will never be enough to relieve your annoyance. This situation will not be unexpected, nor will it be rare. You must have enough experience to know just how many tables you should set aside for your room guests. This problem generally occurs, and is more difficult to resolve, when the hotel restaurant is owned and/or operated by a third party, who is anxious to maximise profit. The customer from outside the hotel, who may be there to splurge on an evening out, may be far more lucrative from the hotel guest who is looking for beans on toast, so herein lies a definite conflict of interest. Although this conflict is between the restaurant operator and the hotel operator, it is the hotel guest, who pays the price.

To overcome this problem most hotels have developed the ubiquitous coffee shop, where fine dining is banished.

Then there is cold food; that is to say food that is supposed to be hot that is served up tepid. The more time chefs take to make a dish look like a spectacular work of art, the greater the risk that, by the time it reaches the dining table, it will no longer be piping hot. That is annoying, notwithstanding that some of the fault may be customers who spend the first five minutes after the plate has arrived, taking pictures of it on their cell phones. I don't really understand why people use cell phones in restaurants as it is so irritating to others, or maybe they are just irritating to me. I once thought that meal times were an opportunity for social contact and interaction. The fact that half of the diners in a restaurant are on cell phones and not talking to each other seems a shame. A lone diner shouting down his phone is just plain annoying.

The quality and price of food and beverage served in a hotel restaurant is a subject for another book. But, outside of the actual wares there are certain unnecessary practices in restaurants that will irritate your hotel guests, that is if they can get into your restaurant without a reservation. A view straight in to the kitchen from the restaurant tables is not normally a good idea unless it has been planned that way. Diners can be quite fascinated to see the inner workings of a kitchen from their table but don't just want a spasmodic view of the dishwashing area as the doors swing open and closed. Nor do diners, on arrival at the restaurant door, want to see a sea of tables, unevenly covered, with unsightly table legs. Table settings must be uniformly applied so that the vision from the door and other tables is attractive. Tables that are too small for the crockery or crockery that is too big for the tables is annoying, especially if there is no space to put down a wine glass or a side dish. If you know that certain menu items won't fit on the tables, change the menu or the tables!

When a table has been vacated, apply some planned relaying method. Otherwise, as the restaurant empties, the remaining diners will feel that they are keeping the staff up. When a diner has finished with a cocktail at the table, don't leave the empty glass there until desert time. Don't clear away a diners plate until the whole party have finished. Serve ladies before men – it might offend some people but will be appreciated by most. Don't ask diners if they are enjoying their meal if they haven't even started; you will sound like a parrot. Fix wobbly tables! Finally, for the umpteenth time, make sure that the air conditioning is not blasting out at your diners and that they can't hear each other talking because the sound system is.

7. The coffee shop

Many hotels with a fine dining restaurant will supplement it with a coffee shop or less refined dining area. The range of these is enormous from twenty-four hour service to breakfast only and from full service to vending machines. Since the standards that are aimed for are generally quite basic there is less room for complaint, as long as the hotel guest gets what he expects and that expectancy is not high. The coffee shop may double for the breakfast room and much of what has been said in the section 'Breakfast Room' will apply, and it would be redundant to repeat it here. The normal principle of a hotel coffee shop is that it is open, not just for breakfast, lunch and dinner, but also for morning coffees, late breakfasts, afternoon teas, early dinners and late-night snacks. This ever-open policy can be difficult to cover in terms of supervision and during busy periods the maintenance of standards can be quite difficult. If not watched constantly, standards of tidiness and hygiene can fall, so it is important that managers and their assistants make frequent trips to this area.

8. The Bar

Hotel guests go to bars for many reasons, but one of them is because they are lonely. Many city hotels have very high single occupancy. This means that most of the guests staying have nobody to talk to. Human beings are not like that. So where can they go to talk to someone but the hotel bar? They can't pick on someone checking in at the lobby, they can't barge into the restaurant and start up a conversation with the diners, but they can sit on a barstool and chat away with the bartender or the other stool sitters. They do not go to the bar because they are thirsty. They go to the bar because they are human beings – 'people who need people'. A good bartender will be a key player in making sure that your guests feel welcome and at home. A good bartender is worth more than a fistful of hotel sales personnel. It is, therefore, particularly annoying to find that many motels don't have a bar, or that it is closed, or that it doesn't have bar stools. Just as breakfast is the focus point of guest activity in the early morning, a good hotel bar will be the focus point in the evening. An efficient but personable bartender can become the real host for the hotel. A good bartender is worth his weight in whiskey. After all, the mere action of pouring a drink for someone is a very sociable act, so it is vital that this role is fulfilled with a member of staff with exceptionally well-honed social skills. Perhaps it would be good for every hotel manager to spend an hour each evening behind the bar? Or, if you are a fairly small operation, why not consider an honour bar where guests just help themselves and mark down what they have taken? Trusting your guests also makes them feel wanted and they will come back – or, if they can't do that, will certainly recommend your place to others. Hotel companies spend so much money on advertising and promoting their wares with sales managers, advertising agencies and public relations experts, whilst ignoring that the best way to fill a hotel is through satisfying the existing clientele. What nicer way to do this than through a friendly bar?

What could be annoying about a bar? After all, if ever there was a place to be jolly and sociable, it should be at the bar. Well, try this for a few: cold beers served in warm glasses. It is nice to know that your glass has just been washed but all this tells the customer is that you are dangerously short on glassware. Instead, it is so easy (and appreciated) to serve a lager in a nice frosted glass.

Getting your clients to stay for a while is important. "Do you have any nibbles?" "I'm afraid not, sir. But I can sell you a packet of crisps." How short sighted that is, when there is no question that a good dose of salt only leads to more drinking. Make sure that the barstools are comfortable and that a sitter is not constantly banged into from behind by a bar waiter. Make sure that the view over the bar is clean and tidy. Yes, it can be workmanlike, because it is a bar, but it should not look like a wet, dirty, mess.

Then there is "where do we sit?" The furnishings in so many hotel bars seem to be such that it is difficult for groups of people to gather comfortably in a sociable manner. Bars are going to be meeting places for social groups. Take a look at your furniture arrangements. Does your furniture lay out and style facilitate constant change as the size of the group of your imbibers fluctuates? Probably not. Finally, as always, there is the music. If this is too loud, or badly selected, your guests will need to raise their voices and, as they partake in a couple of drinks, they will get louder still. This may suit them, but it certainly will not please the rest of your clientele. Keep the background music where it needs to be – in the background.

9. The public toilets

There was a time when I used to inspect the toilets before I sat down at a restaurant table. I often wished I could do that before I get on to an aeroplane. The condition of the public rest rooms in a hotel or restaurant tells you a great deal about the people who operate them, obviously in terms of their hygiene standards, but also in terms of their attention to detail. A badly equipped or maintained loo may not mean that the kitchen operates unhygienically, but it certainly is a bad advert for the business and offers some clues as to the practices of the owners. Public toilets, in terms of their design and physical condition, are an extremely important issue. They are a frequent cause of dissatisfaction. There are rare instances where the décor of the facility is so spectacular that the loo has been elevated to a cause for satisfaction, though not in the physical sense.

It is essential that public restrooms are frequently inspected because people can behave badly in the privacy or these quarters. As well as the regular and frequent cleaning schedule make sure that such things as door hinges, cubicle support structures and so on are thoroughly cleaned. Take a seat from time to time and see what you can see; it will be different from just sticking your head in the door.

10. The gardens and grounds

If you are running a city hotel that has a garden or a resort with extensive grounds then you must understand that it is an extremely important part of your product. During the design and build process the surroundings of the hotel or resort must never be an afterthought. When the list of consultants is drawn up to work on the project, it should always include a landscape designer, even though landscaping is probable one of the last pre-opening activities. Good landscaping can save a fortune on exterior architecture or embellishment. Great landscaping can transform a mundane exterior of a hotel into a wonderland. Because of its purpose, a hotel building is going to have long blocks of buildings with rather uniform sets of doors and windows. It is hard to articulate such blocks architecturally unless a great deal of structural embellishment is applied, which can be very expensive and time consuming. The answer to this problem is frequently in landscaping, and it is, therefore, crucial for the landscape designer and the hotel architect to share the same vision. When we think of the great buildings in the world, we also think of their landscaped surroundings. The Taj Mahal and the Palace of Versailles would not be the same without their gardens, ponds and fountains. So, the planning and development of the gardens and outside spaces of a hotel are crucially important in the overall design.

It is often a shame, therefore, to find, once a hotel has been commissioned and is operating, that the same love and care applied by the landscape designer is often not followed up by hotel management. Hotel guests love to walk in the grounds, if nothing else to relieve themselves from the monotony of a hotel room. Hotel managers, it would seem, are not always the same, and I would venture that very few of them actually 'walk' the outdoors of their premises on a daily basis. And when they do, are they just walking, or are they walking and seeing? It is most annoying, as a hotel guest, to find ill-defined pathways, a multitude of weeds, litter, abandoned gardening equipment and broken fences on a stroll around the grounds. It is also not necessary to catch views, on one's stroll, of untidy back of house areas, such as loading bays, garbage dumps, piles of broken hotel furniture, including kitchen equipment and furniture. Such offerings are often available for the strolling hotel guest who sees what the manager obviously hasn't.

Should your hotel have a golf course and/or tennis courts, remember they are part of the hotel and, for certain guests, the place where they might spend a good portion of their time. As well as for the condition of golf course, you will also be judged by the refreshments offered, either at the eighteenth, the ninth or from a refreshment cart. Don't allow these offerings to be an afterthought, or, in some cases, no thought at all. The condition and presentation of every item of refreshment is a reflection on the standard of your hotel. An untidy driving range or unswept, uneven, tennis courts is one way you will be judged.

Gardens at night can be enchanting; they can also be a liability. When your hotel was first opened there was probably a great deal of attention given to the landscape and pathway lighting. Lights would (or should) have been installed and directed at various features such as trees and shrubs. However, trees and shrubs grow and change. From time to time they die and are replaced. Too often the lighting plan reflects the past and not the present since adjustments are not made as the garden changes. Too often lights that were designed to illuminate pathways or signage are no longer effective. In some resorts, where the only way one can get to the guest rooms is through a garden, the lighting on foot ways is simply inadequate. A sure sign to a guest that 'nobody cares' is missing lightbulbs.

11. Garage and parking

In city hotels, some of your guests will need to park; in roadside hotels they will almost all need to park. A car can often be one of the most valuable assets owned by your guest and, as a result, it should be treated with respect. Many hotels, especially those with limited garage/parking will insist on parking the car for you, quite often because the space is difficult to access or because cars need to be double-banked. In these circumstances the tentative hand that passes a parking ticket to you is waiting for a tip, as is the one that hands you back your key when you retrieve the vehicle. It can be quite annoying, however, to be made to feel awkward when you don't have small notes to hand on these occasions – especially since you are entrusting your prized possession to a man in uniform. It can be doubly annoying when, on check out, you get a bill for parking that is nothing short of gouging. When a person is paying triple figures for accommodation, nickel and diming them on ancillary services, such as parking, is not always smart. When using valet parking (sometimes because there is no alternative), a really feel-good factor is that the car is returned the next day in sparkling clean condition. Most cars will have been on a journey to get to the hotel and will probably be dirty or dusty. I recently stayed in a well-known luxury country house hotel. The drive way to the hotel was loose gravel. My car was quite clean when I arrived at the gates of the hotel grounds but, by the time I had reached the front door, it was covered with dust, as where all the other cars parked there. When I was handed back the keys in the morning my car was still covered in dust. I had just paid over $600 for a room. Would you not have thought that all cars left in the care of the hotel should be washed overnight? They also took my key (for 'safekeeping') but forgot to lock the car.

Self-parking should not present too many difficulties, pro-vided that the spaces are clearly marked and that there is an obvious and smooth route to wheel your luggage to the, hopefully, well signed check-in area. One of the first con-cerns in the guest pyramid of needs is safety and security. This does not only apply to hotel bedroom doors but also to the security of your car and its contents. A well-lit and well patrolled car park is, therefore, essential.

12. The pool

To some extent the hotel swimming pool has become the outdoor focal point to compare with the main, inside, lobby. The pool, for many, is also a meeting point; a place to be seen and, perhaps more importantly, to see. There is normally plenty to see at the pool and often there are plenty of people willing to show. A well designed and visually appealing pool area is essential to the success of a resort hotel. It must offer comfort by way of loungers, shaded areas, tables; these should be arranged in a visually attractive pattern, before they are moved about by guests for socialising or privacy. Many of your hotel bedrooms will look down at the pool area, so it is important that it looks visually attractive from above. Naturally the pool, itself, must be sparkling clean. The depth markings must be clear and the 'rules' clearly displayed. The manager of the pool area is as important as the maître d' in the restaurant. This task should not be left to an amateur or elevated life guard. The pool manager must get to know the likes, dislikes, whims and service requirements of all of his guests; after all, he is probably going to see them every day and all day (in some cases) for at least a week, and maybe on many return visits. A pool service manager, who acts as a host, is vital to giving your guests a memorable vacation. He must be diplomatic in sorting out the land grabs of the pool area (i.e. 'ownership' of loungers, towels, etc.), he must make sure that refreshments are swiftly served without the guest having to venture off the sunbed, and he must be vigilant in keeping the place spic and span. And all of this with a smile. Without this attention to detail and personal needs, pool areas can become very unpleasant. Territorial arguments can break out, noisy screaming children can terrorise the place, voices raised through the consumption of too many glasses of gin can be aggravating and excessively rambunctious games on the pool can be dangerous, as can spilt beverages or ice creams.

A hotel swimming pool occupies a large space; it must therefore be designed to look attractive and to complement the architecture of the establishment. However, the design of some pools, means that they are more decorative than useful. They are often situated close to restaurants and bars, where the sparkling water enhances the ambience of the dining facility, especially in the evening. These pools are not designed for laps or water polo, so alternatives should be offered. A bunch of noisy children, gleefully shouting at each other next to the dining room can be annoying.

It is crucial that you see your pool as your biggest physical asset and one, therefore, that needs continuous supervision and management. By definition, the pool, other than purely those for exercising, is the place where your clientele will spend much of their vacation. Many of them will see things that you will miss on a whistle-stop visit. Many of them will wonder why 'management doesn't notice these things'. If you take the time to stop and talk to your guests every day at poolside you will, not only be cementing return business, but you will also find out and see, what is going wrong.

13. The beach

If your hotel offers a beach from which swimming is permissible then it must be viewed by management as an operational facility of the hotel. This service should stretch to the availability of beach towels, shaded areas and beach furniture. If possible, beverage service should be made available and even little luxury touches like cleaning sun glasses will make a difference. Establish a system whereby your guests can summon service when they need it, rather than constantly bothering them. Many hoteliers don't seem to understand that the beach is often the reason guests have selected your hotel. Just look at how resort chains advertise; the beach is always prominent in the advert – so don't ignore your guests who spend half their days there.

Beach niggles often revolve around things that are difficult to control, such as beach vendors, noisy surf riders and so on, but through cooperation with your local administrations these can often be marginalised.

In some cases, beach games organised by the hotel staff are well received but make sure that there are always quiet areas available. Avoid piped music actually on the beach because nature produces its own music with waves crashing and birds singing. However, the occasional musical concert, taped or otherwise, possibly at sunset, can be a very romantic attraction.

Make facilities available for children, otherwise they can be very annoying to guests that don't have them, or didn't bring them. Create a separate play area for kids, either on or near the beach, or near the pool area. Happy children mean happy parents.

Most of all, keep your beach clean. A dirty, litter-strewn beach is a great cause for annoyance. Before your first guest stakes her claim by laying down her towel in the sand, your stretch of beach should have been raked clean.

If you operate a boathouse with small craft available for guests, it is essential, of course, that these are kept in pristine condition; likewise, for scuba and fishing equipment. And boathouse people can be untidy; so make sure that it is not left off the manager's 'rounds'.

14. Uniforms

Most hotel staff need to, or are required to, wear a uniform, if for no other purpose than to indicate to the guest that they are service personnel. In some cases, this uniform involves nametags. These are useful to guests who wish to address staff by name, but that is completely negated if the print on the nametags is unreadable, which is often the case. Uniforms should make employees feel good, not ridiculous. They should also be practical and appropriate for the job. The design and condition of staff uniforms is critical to upholding the quality and image of your establishment. Dirty uniforms translate into 'dirty hotel'. Tired, threadbare uniforms translate into 'tired, threadbare hotel'. A uniform, properly designed, gives an indication to a guest of what a staff member is supposed to do or what position they hold in the place. The issue and control of uniforms is an extremely important function; making sure that they are properly laundered and pressed. But, even when uniform design and control are exceptionally well arranged there is an Achilles Heel, and it is right at the heel. Normally shoes and socks are not part of the issued uniform, for obvious reasons. This should not mean that they are beyond the control of hotel management. Even the smartest uniform can be ruined by dirty, down at heel, shoes and/or the wrong colour socks. It is not an infringement on the civil liberties of employees to point out to them that they are not maintaining the high standards you have set by telling them to clean their shoes or change their socks. Install a shoe cleaning machine in the back of house. There is little use in operating an elegantly or efficiently designed hotel with a bunch of scruffs.

15. Cleanliness

Impeccable hygiene in a hotel is, of course, absolute essential. You would think that it was redundant to write these words. Of course, everybody understands that the biggest 'dissatisfier' of all would be a dirty hotel. But, regrettably, accidents do happen and surfaces do get soiled. In some cases, unfortunately this is not by accident, but simply bad behaviour on the part of guests, who do not treat your hotel as if it were their home – or maybe they do. A worn hotel is annoying; a dirty hotel is unacceptable. You will, therefore, need to be vigilant in regard to stained carpets, bedspreads, linens, drapes etc. Not only will you need to take ongoing remedial action vis-à-vis spills and mishaps as they occur or are noticed or reported, but you should also institute a planned carpet and fabric cleaning process. This may be one job that can safely be handled by contract with a specialist.

Keeping public areas clean is a different matter. These areas are often lit with mood lighting which makes it quite difficult to see dirt or stains. In the planning process make sure that you have the capability from time to time (probably in the middle of the night) to switch on flood lighting which shows up every nook and cranny, so that they can be thoroughly cleaned. Even a late-night reveller, upon returning to a floodlit lobby will appreciate the fact that cleaning must be done. You, the manager, and your assistants can play a big part in the hygiene effort because you have the freedom, right and need to walk around all of the property frequently. On these rounds, hygiene should be uppermost in your mind. Make a habit of checking out those awkward corners that cleaners often miss. Remember that you don't see everything from eye level when you are walking along. From time to time get down on your haunches or climb up on some steps. Your employees will soon get the message.

"I booked a junior suite so that we would have a little more space, since we were going to be in town for a few days. Between us we had two suitcases and two small pull-alongs, which had fitted into the overhead racks on the plane. The porter brought the bags to the room and then left. He made no attempt to find us a luggage rack or anything. We could see why; because there simply was nowhere to put the bags to unpack, except on the bed. This was the most badly designed room; I could have done better myself."

– 'DISSATISFIED', LONDON

"Why do I need a view of the manager's office every time I arrive at the front door? His office looks such a mess, especially at night. Wouldn't you think someone could have designed things better?"

– MRS JAMES BRIGHT, ANDOVER

"It is very difficult to get one's bags to the rooms; there are too many steps and bumps on the route and it is quite a steep climb. You should have a baggage service."

– JEREMY CAMPER, YORK, UK

"At the desk they told me they had upgraded me to a mountain view room. Actually, between my balcony and the mountains is the sewage treatment plant!"

– ALEX SWEETWATER, CHRISTCHURCH, NZ

"It was impossible to get a good night's sleep. The walls between the rooms are paper thin. I could hear every word the people in the next room were saying and they seemed to talk all night."

– ANNE SHARP, DUBAI

Chapter Six
Design and Construction

As you read this booklet, I have no doubt that you will be thinking that the cause of many of the annoyances mentioned will be the design of the hotel. I can hear you saying that there is nothing you can do about many of them because they are caused by built-in factors, and changing them could be very expensive. It is true that, in some cases, what is done is done, but a close look may reveal that there are post-construction solutions. The best time to make sure that these problems are eliminated is, of course, in the design stage, particularly very early into the programme. For this reason, it is essential that operational staff and management are involved in the planning team right from the conception of the product. However, the 'ops' team input into the plans must be exceptionally thorough; not just a quick flip through the plans. As an operations manager your input into the planning process must be thoughtful, thorough and extremely detailed. You may also need to be very forceful because designers and architects can be heavily invested into their plans and ideas and, as a result, not easy to move. Hotel developers will have a high respect for the consultants' opinions (after all, they are paying them a lot), so you will need to be very strong and logical with yours.

It is sometimes quite hard to visualise a three-dimensional item when it is only displayed to you on a flat piece of paper. For this reason, you must insist that the drawings are turned into pictorial renderings and even small scale models. This is expensive, but the renderings, at least can be easily produced on a computer. Start your analysis of the project with the plans. Try to imagine you are actually in the room or space that is drawn. Examine every aspect. Check that the furniture has been drawn to the right scale. Check that the doors have actually been drawn to the correct size. Check the ceiling height. Question the partition soundproofing that is planned. Measure the spaces and envisage yourself therein. Ask questions such as "What happens when this wall joins this ceiling?" "What will this corner look like?" "What can I see from this window?" "Is the closet wide enough to take a hanger with a coat on it?" "Where is the air conditioning unit or fan?" "Where are the maid's rooms?"

Take the plans and imagine a guest going through the pattern of a stay. Start at the front gate and walk through the plan as if you are actually there. Ask where the valet service will work from, what route will the luggage take to a room, where luggage trolleys will be stored, where left luggage can be stored and so on until you have 'imagined' the processes of a complete guest stay from arrival, feeding, sleeping, drinking to departure. This is a long process but an essential one. After all, you or your operational team are going to have to make this thing work. The last thing you want to do is to spoil the architectural and design impact of the potential building, but, as we have seen, your will need to eliminate the 'dissatisfiers' before you can reach the 'satisfiers'. In other words, the plans and the drawings might look spectacular but if the hotel will not function it will all be for naught.

This process of analysing plans will tend to have a couple of phases. The first only involves architectural and engineering; the second will include the furnishing, décor and landscaping. The biggest mistakes need to be corrected at the architectural plans stage. If, for example, the lobby space is just too small to be able to function, or if the restaurant space is not capable of holding your inhouse guests, or the corridors are too narrow, or the loading bay can be seen from the porte cochere, then this must be addressed at the outset and it must be addressed before earthworks and foundations can commence. Challenge the planned arrival experience. Is it immediately in your face or is it a process of discovery? Check the actual siting or the building. Have the architects placed it in exactly the right place for maximisation of the view in the arrival experience or from the rooms and suites? Often the moving of a building by twenty feet, or the skewing of it to show off the sites best aspects can make a huge difference to its impact. Many architects work on the drawing board rather than on the actual site. For this reason, when planning a new hotel or resort development it is essential that the full team of consultants is hired and involved before any building work starts. This team must include operational personnel. Amazingly, this does not always happen.

Once the shape and scope of the actual construction has been agreed and work commenced, the interior and exterior design teams will be able to start detailed work. The devil is in the detail. At this stage you will be asked frequently "Do you like the way this looks?" and your opinion will be valuable. However, your question should be "how does it work?" "How do I clean it?" "How do you change a light bulb?" and so on. In proposed public areas this can be a difficult process because it requires leaps of imagination, but now is the time to ask practical questions so that they can be incorporated into the design, not tacked on afterwards with makeshift solutions.

Bedroom design is somewhat different because one can mock up a room in a warehouse to test its visual appeal and practicality. Building a mock up bedroom is essential, but utilising it constructively is extremely important. First, try to build it in a place that is easily accessible to all of the people that should review it. It does not need to be on site. Second, make sure that it is real. It must be precisely the size as drawn on the plans and must contain all of the finishes, fixtures and fittings that are proposed by the design team. No excuses, like "This is only a sample shower control; the real one is on order." The people reviewing must review what is proposed, not something close to it. That said, make sure that all of the right people get to see the mock-up and that you closely evaluate, consider and action what is suggested. I remember many years ago being invited by an airline, on which I was a frequent flyer, to evaluate, along with other frequent flyers, a proposed new business class seat design, which had been mocked up in their offices. The assembled group was quite unanimous about its faults but, a year later, the seat was introduced into all of their planes exactly as it had been when we critiqued it. What was the point?

The right people to look at the hotel mock-up are all of the people who will need to service it, as well as potential users. The 'users' could be pulled from frequent guests or your marketing department, but the 'servicers' must include the housekeeping staff (both senior and maid level), hotel man-agement, sales and marketing personnel and maintenance engineers. Those asked will feel proud (and involved) that they have been. However, don't do this as a group exercise.

Let each reviewer have time to try things, feel things and contemplate. Encourage them to imagine themselves staying in the room, trying the TV set, controlling the shower, storing their luggage, hanging their clothes, and so on. Give them some sort of form to fill in, but don't lead them by the nose and set the parameters too strictly. Let them look at the room and consider it from their point of view. This process is vital. It is also your only chance to tweak things before good money is spent. Remember, those that designed it will have 'ownership' of the design. They will defend it. They will not necessarily want to change what they have done. You will need to grasp the balance between good looks and practicality. Make sure that the mock-up is not destroyed as soon as it has been used. Certain changes will need to be made after the critique. These should be incorporated into the mock-up as they are sourced to make sure that they are right. The mock-up may also be used as a tool for the marketing department.

Whilst a great deal of thought is often put into the design of hotel bedrooms by the operations team, the hotel suites and penthouses often slip by them unnoticed, because it is impractical to mock up every 'special' case. This can be a great shame because the suites of a hotel are often, not only the highest revenue producers per square foot, but are also an ongoing advert for the property as a whole. Interior designers love to play around with sexy suite design; it tends to become their calling card. Unfortunately, they do not often stay in them to experience their impracticalities, nor do they have to figure out how to clean them. Without taking away from the design intent and impact, it is extremely important for operators to take a close look at suite design and intended materials, before big money is spent. Likewise, it is impossible to mock up restaurants and interior design companies tend to produce renderings and plans that have too much artistic licence. It is incumbent, therefore, on hotel management to take a close look at these plans whilst they are still plans, not after the tables and chairs have been ordered. It is also important to check that the table configurations and sizes, as drawn on the plans are actually the same as the ones that are to be ordered and used. Also, important is to examine the height of banquet seating to make sure that future customers are not sitting in a hole. Likewise, kitchen plans need great scrutiny. These planning services are often provided by kitchen equipment suppliers, but, guess what, they are also likely to be selling you the goods, so take care that you are not ordering things that you don't actually need.

"I had a lovely stay at your resort; everything was wonderful. And the manager was so good; he was always friendly and attentive. I could see that he always had his eyes about him. I will certainly go back. Thankyou."

– PEACHES GOODFELLA, TRENTON, NJ

"I stayed at your resort for ten days. I never saw the manager once. In my business I am always on the shop floor to give encouragement and to make sure that things are going right. Why don't hotel managers do this? I could tell them a thing or two about what goes on."

– JACK LABOUR, SWANSEA, WALES

"I notice that the best table in the restaurant is reserved for the manager."

– 'DISENCHANTED', EPPING, LONDON

"A lot of your guests are businessmen. It is hard for a businessman to switch off and relax. Whilst sitting at your pool or bar, we tend to want to reorganise things. We see things that you don't. Why? Because you don't stick around long enough to see anything!"

– SIMON OVERSTRAND, GENEVA

Chapter Seven
Solutions

Taken separately, the whinges and ideas enumerated in this book must seem pretty inconsequential and petty. Most of them, taken alone, would not add up to a spoiled stay or a reason never to return. However, their cumulative effect could be just so – a lost customer. Too many lost customers result in lost revenue and extra marketing costs to attract new business. Just how many of the 100-plus niggles listed in this book will it take for someone to stay away is anyone's guess – but the less reasons there are to complain, the better.

To understand the nature of dissatisfaction and satisfaction in regard to our hotel guests it is helpful to take a broader look at human nature. At the very basic level human beings need sustenance; without sufficient food and drink they will not survive. When this need is satisfied, the human being needs to feel safe. There is no good having a full belly if you are going to get mugged, murdered or sick. Safety includes a safe place to stay – a roof over your head with a front door and windows that can be secured. Living in a secure place with a roof over one's head and protected from the elements is okay, but if you have nobody to share it with, it can be lonely and depressing. Humans are gregarious; they need from time to time to be in contact with others. They are also greedy; once they have something, they tend to want something more – i.e. a bigger house, a more comfortable house, a television set, a washing machine and so on. Soon they want to live at a better address and have a Mercedes in the garage. They want to be perceived as successful. But these things count for naught, unless they have meaningful personal relationships and a fulfilling role or occupation.

Hotels reflect much of this pyramid of needs. First of all, the hotel must be safe and secure. Proper lighting, located in a good neighbourhood, a lock on the bedroom door are all essential. The hotel must meet the basic needs of shelter and comfort. However, once these needs are met, it must meet the other human needs of the guest. A full stomach, a place to impress, a place to socialise, a place to say that you have 'arrived'.

Broadly speaking there are a whole bunch of things that a hotel must get right in order not to cause dissatisfaction. They tend to be in the lower range of human needs. If the hotel is dirty, or in an unsafe area, or badly lit, the guests will be dissatisfied. If all of these things are not an issue, the hotel guest will not be satisfied; he will just not be dissatisfied. If a hotel room has an uncomfortable bed, hard, small towels or no hot water, the guest will be dissatisfied. If the reverse is true and the bed is comfortable, the towels are a good size and the water is hot, he will not be dissatisfied; nor will he be satisfied, because these are things that he expects. We are not satisfied when we get things that we expect; we are satisfied when we get things beyond our expectancies. We are satisfied when people recognise us, when they go the extra mile for us, when they are kind to us and so on. Interestingly, the 'satisfiers' are often the things that cost little to give, whereas the dissatisfiers often are due to a lack of effective expenditure.

That said, most annoyances can be corrected and dealt with easily. But first, management has to recognise that they are there and then plan corrective action. How can a hotel manager find out what is annoying his guests?

Here are a few simple steps that every hotel manager should follow. In fact, they are so simple, that one hesitates to state them because they seem so obvious. However, they do come down to discipline, particularly self- discipline, and we all know how easily this can slide. So, here are a few disciplines that hotel managers should adopt on a frequent and regular basis.

1. Stay in your own hotel

Make a point of regularly staying overnight in your own hotel. Make a reservation through your hotel website or one of the many online booking services. Find out just how efficient they are – or are not. Take note of any booking sites that are frustrating and, later, after, ask them to take corrective action.

Sometimes stay at the hotel for a couple of nights, so that you can get a feel of consistency of service, but on each new visit always stay in different rooms. From time to time stay in a suite, but don't fall into the trap of always opting for the most comfortable or grand accommodation; this is not a vacation. By ringing the changes, you will experience different noises, different odours, different views and so on. Behave exactly as a guest would. Bring luggage, use the closet, the safe, the minibar, the laundry. Try room service. Ask for a special pillow.

Make a careful note of everything that is irritating, everything that goes wrong and everything that goes right. If there are physical or maintenance items that need fixing, initiate the necessary action. You can be fairly sure that the things happening to you in your 'test' room will be happening elsewhere in the hotel. Keep a careful list of these items and monitor later their correction progress.

Don't be worried about asking your wife, husband, or partner to join you. Two pairs eyes are often better than one and a view from the other sex can be different and helpful. Be aware that the staff will know who you are and that you will probably be getting special treatment, so take account of the fact that everyone may not have it so good. Nevertheless, you will still learn plenty about the standards being operated.

As often as you can, make a point of staying in other hotels, either competitors or others within the company that you work for. It has always seemed odd to me that hotel managers, and their families, are not necessarily welcomed guests in their colleagues' hotels. This is something which should be facilitated with extra special rates by the company. Not only might a visiting manager learn something, she is in a perfect position to give meaningful feedback to a colleague. Staying in competitors' hotels, of course, is not to find fault, but to find inspiration. Most hotel entrepreneurs will have had a good hard look at the opposition before spending millions on development. Why not make sure that hotel managers have the same learning opportunities?

There has been a proliferation of hotel schools, colleges and universities around the globe over the last fifty years. Clearly this has been helpful in raising the profile of the industry as well as the standards. However, learning in a hotel school has one enormous drawback; most of the teaching staff have had very little exposure to staying in hotels, particularly hotels that are expensive. Although many teachers are theoretically excellent, their practical exposure is normally very limited. Plenty of them will have worked in the hotel industry, but, the fact that they have become teachers rather than practitioners, would seem to indicate that they may not have been hugely successful at the coalface. This may not be a problem in teaching accounting or purchasing, or even culinary skills, but it definitely is a drawback in regard to providing exceptionally good hotel services. After all, if you have never been a guest yourself, how do you translate the experience to others? One would hope that the hotel industry would recognise this flaw in the system and come up with plans to facilitate 'hotel guest experience' to all those that are teaching it. The feedback might be good in both directions.

2. Manage by walking (or riding) around

Although the process of managing a hotel requires attention to plenty of paperwork, the manager's office must not become a haven. The more that a manager is out and about the premises the more he will see, the more he will learn and the more he can improve. Surveys have shown that the first thing most hotel managers do upon arrival each morning is to head for the office and call for a cup of coffee. As mentioned earlier in this booklet the best place a manager can be, first thing in the morning, is in the breakfast room, because that's where most of his guests are. The mail and other paperwork can wait. Being there, to watch what goes on with the service, particularly when it is at its busiest, is invaluable. When service is stretched the cracks appear. Not enough staff, not enough equipment, not enough restaurant seats, and so on. You won't see this in the office. You may see its effect in reading departed guests' surveys but, by then, it is far too late. There is no substitute for being there.

Also, as we have seen earlier, the majority of your guests will also be 'there', and this is probably the only period of the day that they will. It is therefore a perfect time for your presence to be noticed and for your concerns to be displayed. It also gives you the chance to pick up valuable feedback about your guest's stay and to take corrective action, if required, whilst they are still in house.

There are other times in the day, when the service is not under strain, for you to do the office work or to hold meetings with your department heads or staff. And not all meetings with your supervisors have to take place in your office. Instead of calling the chef to your office, go to his. You will learn much more about what is going on than from behind your desk. Also, make yourself a promise; that you will always interrupt a meeting with employees to attend to a call to meet a guest or sort out a guest relations matter. It may be infuriating to those attending the meeting that you jump up in the middle of it, to go to the lobby to meet an arriving guest on a return visit, but it will send the right message.

A hotel manager should spend several hours a day outside his office, sometimes in the front and sometimes at the back. A manager should 'walk' his property, both inside and out, on different routes every day, armed with notepad or recording gizmo. She should get to know the names of her staff at all levels, both in the front of house and in the bowels of the building. A walkabout manager will see first-hand the chaos at the loading bay, smell the stink in the garbage room, catch the admin staff playing computer games, witness the room service trays in the hallway from the night before. She will also see and overhear staff doing the right thing, going the extra mile. None of this can be done from the office. By being out there, managers will already see what they will read in graphs and charts, or quest surveys, AFTER the event.

3. Meet your guests

In 1972, Shelley Berman described the Hotel Manager, who is pictured hiding behind his office chair, as follows:

"He's out of his office right now.
He's in a meeting.
He's not in yet.
He's out to lunch.
Do not hesitate to call if he can be of any assistance.
Or contact the Assistant Manager."

The Assistant Manager (also hiding behind his office chair):
"He's out of his office right now.
He's in a meeting.
He's expected momentarily.
He's out to lunch.
Do not hesitate to call him of he can be of any assistance."

Absolutely the best feedback about the quality and value of your standards and service will come from the people who are paying for it. You can get this in several ways. Either from written or online questionnaires from departed guests, from reports from your assistants and employees, or directly from them to you. The last is the most profitable source of information; it also incorporates feelings. You can reply to guest survey feedback in writing, text or phone. You can ask your assistants to do it for you. But nothing works as well as the person to person interaction. I once worked for the manager of a hotel which had about 100 arrivals per day. Each morning he took the arrival list and underlined ten names. He then copied the list and sent it in rotation to ten supervisors on his team, including those with potentially direct access to guests, but also some from the back of house, such as the chef, the engineer and the accountant. In each case he asked them to underline ten additional names. The idea was that each supervisor should attempt to meet or talk to or leave message for, their ten choices. What this meant was that, every day, all 100 arrivals were met by or contacted by a senior member of staff, with a welcome and an offer of direct line access, should they need something during their stay. Not everybody achieved 100% contact every day, but the discipline rammed home the importance of the guest, rather than the importance of the particular function each of us thought we were performing. The feedback from guests was amazingly useful and, in some cases, humbling. The goodwill that was created was invaluable.

As mentioned earlier, the breakfast room is a good place to meet guests; you are fishing where the fish are. But there are other opportunities, depending upon the nature of your hotel. Poolside at a resort in the day, or the cocktail bar at happy hour are good spots. One of the best however is at the check- out. If you can make contact with a few people per day as they leave, one of the lasting impressions they will have of your hotel will be the friendly face of management wishing them au revoir. And, if they are leaving, for whatever reason, on a sour note, this is your last chance to sweeten them.

There will also be some side benefits from actually meeting your guests, other than picking up the feedback, good or bad, from their experiences. By definition you will be 'out there', watching and seeing what is happening, witnessing your staff in action and noting if your systems are working. By being there you can pick up the things that will annoy your guests and initiate corrective action. You will not have to wait for a paper report on this in a month's time.

Appendix One
Can't Get 'No Satisfaction'

During the course of writing this book I have referred on several occasions to the difference between the 'satisfiers' and 'dissatisfiers', as they relate to hotel guests. I thought it might be useful, in this regard, to reprint below a portion of my book *Managing Hotels*, published in 1983, which examines the concept of satisfaction and dissatisfaction as it pertains to hotel service.

Can't get 'no satisfaction'

While Abraham Maslow's theories of the needs of human beings seem to relate closely to the needs of hotel guests, so do the findings of another famous industrial behavioural researcher – Frederick Herzberg.

Herzberg is best known for his hygiene/motivation theory which is widely taught in man-management classes. The classical approach to motivation, according to Herzberg, has concerned itself with the environment in which the employee works; i.e. the circumstances that surround him while he works and things that he is given in exchange for his work. Herzberg considers this concern with the environment to be an ongoing necessity of management, but that is not sufficient in itself for effective motivation. Motivation requires experiences that are inherent in the job itself.

Herzberg maintains that it is impossible to motivate people by using environmental factors, i.e. better conditions of work (he calls them *hygiene* factors). Only through achieving satisfaction from the job itself can people, he maintains, be fully motivated with lasting effect.

He uses the term hygiene to describe such things as physical working conditions, supervising policies, the climate of union-management relations, wages and fringe benefits. Herzberg chose the term *hygiene* to describe these factors because they are essentially preventative from the environment, just as trash removal removes threats to health from the physical environment. His research has shown that when any of these factors are deficient, employees are likely to be displeased and to express their displeasure in ways that hamper the organisation, e.g. through grievances, decrease efforts or even strikes. When deficiencies are corrected productivity may return to normal but is unlikely to rise above that level. In other words, an investment in hygiene may eliminate a deficit, but does not create a gain. As Herzberg says "Just as eating a meal does not prevent a man from becoming hungry in the future, a wage increase will not prevent him from being dissatisfied eventually with his new level of wage."

To sustain higher levels of performance an employee must be motivated and motivation, according to Herzberg, describes the feelings of accomplishment, of professional growth and professional recognition, that are experienced in a job that offers sufficient challenge and scope to a worker.

Thus, Herzberg has illustrated to thousands of managers that 'dissatisfiers' are not the opposite of 'satisfiers' – they are just different. The lesson to be learned from Herzberg's research and theories are, of course, applicable to the management of hotel employees and the structuring of hotel jobs. They do not, however, focus on the parallels of his theory to the satisfaction of hotel guests. It would appear that in regard to guest service there are many things that need to be done to prevent dissatisfaction (i.e. hygiene factors) but these things, if successful, will not necessarily lead to the satisfaction of guests (motivational theories). Many hotel managers spend their time trying to satisfy their guests without understanding the difference between the satisfiers and the dissatisfiers.

For example, do you think that an arriving hotel guest will be dissatisfied if his hotel room is dirty? Of course, he will. On the other hand, do you think an arriving hotel guest will be satisfied if he arrives in a clean room? No – he will just not be dissatisfied! Similarly, whereas the provision of soap and towels does not satisfy the average hotel guest; the lack of soap and towels is certain cause for dissatisfaction.

Below are two questions and extracts from two lists which I have tested informally on many people. Try answering the questions for yourself to see if your own results confirm my experiences which are marked accordingly.

1. The items listed below are all unfavourable aspects of a hotel operation. Give each item a rating as to the amount of dissatisfaction it will cause a guest.

	Dissatisfaction		
	High	Medium	Low
A reservation mix-up upon arrival		x	
Dirty bedroom	x		
Rather sullen staff		x	
Insufficient bathroom linen	x		
Only 'average' food		x	
Staff do not address by name			x
Insufficient hot water supply	x		
Hotel decoration rather ordinary			x
Manager never seen			x
Public areas quite 'dead'		x	

2. The items listed below are all favourable aspects of a hotel operation. Give each item a rating as to the amount of satisfactory impact it would have on a guest.

	Satisfaction		
	High	Medium	Low
A correctly handled reservation			x
A clean room		x	
Ever-smiling courteous staff	x		
Sufficient towels			x
Excellent Food	x		
Many staff remember your name	x		
Sufficient supply of hot water			x
Manager makes contact with guests	x		
The hotel is strikingly decorated		x	
The public areas are lively and full		x	

If your results with this experiment are similar to mine, by overlapping in your mind one list on top of the other, you will have a clear indication about satisfiers from the movement of your markings. This appears to reaffirm the earlier conclusions derived from the work of Herzberg that the satisfiers are not the same thing as the dissatisfiers. Abraham Maslow concluded in his famous research that unless the factors at the lower level of needs are met you have no chance of satisfying the upper level needs. Herzberg concluded, similarly, that unless the hygiene factors, or environmental factors, are dealt with, you have no chance of getting to the stage of benefits from the motivational factors. In regards to hotel management, this seems to be telling us that if we can't get the basics right, we will have no chance of satisfying our guests. On the other hand, if we have got the basics covered, there is another whole level of effort required to have really happy guests.

* * *

The above was written almost forty years ago. Is it still relevant? I believe so. The difference between a hotel that functions well and one that blows away the customer is as important now as it was then. The costs of marketing a hotel or resort are huge. The costs of being friendly to and showing care for your guests are actually quite small.

Appendix Two
Conversation with Room Service
(by the late Shelley Berman)

Reading hints. You are on the phone. The other party is also in the hotel.

Morny, rune sore-bees.
Oh sorry, I thought I had dialled room service.

Rye. Rune sore-bees. Morny. Jewish to odor sunteen?
Yes, order something. This is room thirteen oh five. I want…

Okay, torino-fie. Yes plea?
I'd like some bacon and eggs.

Ow July them?
What?

Aches. Ow July them? Pry, boy, pooch…?
Oh, the eggs! How do I like them! Sorry. Scrambled, please.

Ow July thee baycome? Crease?
Crisp will be fine.

Okay. An Santos?
What?

Santos. July santos?
Uh... I don't know... I don't think so.

No? Judo one toes?
Look, I feel really bad about this, but I just don't know that judo-one-toes means. I'm sorry....

Toess! Toes! Why Jew Don Juan toes? Ow bow eenlish mopping we bother?
Englisn muffin! I've got it! Toast! You were saying toast! Fine. An English muffin will be fine.

We bother?
No, just put the bother on the side.

Wad?
I'm sorry. I meant butter. Butter on the side.

Copy?
I feel terrible about this but...

Copy. Copy, tea, mill...
Coffee! Yes, coffee please. And that's all.

One Minnie. Ass rune torino-fie, strangle aches, crease bayconne, tossy eenlish mopping we bother honey sign, and copy. Rye?
Whatever you say.

Okay. Tenjewberrymud.
You're welcome.

Appendix Three
Free Soap
(by the late Shelley Berman)

Dear Maid,
Please do not leave more of those little bars of soap in my bathroom since I have brought my own bath-size Dial. Please remove the six unopened little bars from the shelf under the medicine chest and another three in the shower soap dish. Thank you.
> S Berman

Dear Room 635,
I am not your regular maid she will be back tomorrow (Thurs) from her day off. I took the 3 hotel soaps out of the shower soap dish as you requested. The 6 bars on your shelf I took out of your way and put on top of your Kleenex dispenser should you change your mind. This leaves only the 3 bars I left today which my instructions from the management is to leave 3 soaps daily I hope this is satisfactory. If anything else comes up please call Mrs Corum in the linen room.
> Kathy (relief maid)

Dear Maid (I hope you are my regular maid),
Apparently, Kathy did not tell you about my note to her concerning the little bars of soap. When I got back to my

room this evening I found you had added 3 little Camays to the shelf under my medicine cabinet. I am going to be here in the hotel for two weeks and have bought my own bath-size Dial so I won't need those 6 little Camays which are now on the shelf. They are in my way when shaving, brushing teeth, etc. Please remove them.

> S Berman

Dear Mr Berman,
My day off was last Wed so the relief maid left 3 hotel soaps which we are instructed by the management. I took the 6 soaps which were in your way on the shelf and put them in the soap dish where your Dial was. I put the Dial in the medicine cabinet for your convenience. I didn't remove the 3 complementary soaps which are always placed inside the medicine cabinet for all new check-ins and which you did not object to when you checked in last Monday. Also I did place 3 hotel soaps on your shelf as per my instructions from the management since you left no instructions to the contrary. Please let me know if I can be of further assistance or call linen room her name is Mrs Korm. Have a pleasant stay.

> Your regular maid, Dotty

Dear Mr Berman,
The assistant manager, Mr Kensedder, informed me this a.m. that your called him last evening to say that you were unhappy with your maid service. I have assigned a new girl to your room. I hope you will accept my apologies for the past inconvenience. If you have any future complaints please contact me so I can give it my personal attention. Call extension 1108 between 8 a.m and 5 p.m. Thank you.

> Elaine Carmen, Housekeeper

Dear Miss Carmen,

It is impossible to contact you by phone since I leave the hotel for business at 7.45 a.m. and don't get back before 5.30 or 6 p.m. That's the reason I called Mr, Kensedder last night. You were already off duty. I only asked Me. Kensedder if he could do anything about those little bars of soap. I did not want a new maid. The new maid you assigned me must have thought I was a new check-in today, since she left another 3 bars of hotel soap in my medicine cabinet along with her regular delivery of 3 bars on the bathroom shelf. In just five days here I have accumulated 24 little bars of soap. I'm beginning to dread the next 9 days. Why are you doing this to me?

     S. Berman

Dear Mr Berman,

Your maid Kathy, has been instructed to stop delivering soap to your room and remove extra soaps. If I can be of further assistance. Please call extension 1108 between 8 am. and 5 p.m. Thank you.

     Elaine Carmen, Housekeeper

Dear Mr Kensedder,

My bath-size Dial is missing. Every bar of soap was taken from my room including my own bath-size Dial. I came in late last night and had to call the bellhop to bring me a bar of soap so I could take a shower. He bought me 4 little Cashmere Bouquets.

     S . Berman

Dear Mr Berman,

I have informed our Housekeeper, Elaine Karmin, of your soap problem. I cannot understand why there was no soap in your room since are maids are instructed to leave three bars of soap each time they service a room. The situation will be rectified immediately. Please accept my apologies for the inconvenience. If you prefer Cashmere Bouquet to Camay, please contact Mrs Karmin on extension 1108. Thank you.

Martin L Kensedder, Assistant Manager.

Dear Mrs Carmen,
Who the hell left 54 little bars of Camay in my room? I came in last night and found 54 little bars of soap. I do not want 54 little bars of Camay. I want my 1 damn bar of bath-size Dial. Do you realise I have 58 bars of soap in here? All I want is my bath-size Dial. Give me back my bath-size Dial.

S Berman

Dear Mr Berman,
You complained of too much soap in your room so I had them removed. You then complained to Mr Kensedder that all your soap was missing so I personally returned them; the 24 Camays which had been taken and 3 Camays you are supposed to receive daily. I do not know anything about the 4 Cashmere Bouquets. Obviously your maid Kathy did not know I had returned you soaps so she brought 24 Camays plus the 2 daily Camays. I do not know where you got the idea that this hotel issues bath-size Dial I was able to locate some hotel-size bath-size Ivory which I left in your room. We are doing our best to satisfy you.

Elaine Carmen, Housekeeper

Dear Mrs Carmen,
Just a short note to bring you up to date on my latest soap inventory. As of today I possess:

On shelf under medicine cabinet: 18 Camay in 4 stacks of 4 and 1 stack of 2.

On Kleencx dispenser: 11 Camay in 2 stacks of 4 and 1 stack of 3

On bedroom dresser: I stack of 3 Cashmere Bouquet, I stack of 4 hotel size Ivory, 8 Camay in 2 stacks of 4.

Inside medicine cabinet: 14 Camay in 3 staccks of 4 and 1 stack of 2.

In shower soap dish: 6 Camay (very moist)

On northeast corner of tub: I Cashmere Bouquet (slightly used).

On northwest corner of tub: 6 Camay in 2 stacks of 3

Please ask Kathy when she services my room to make sure the stacks are neatly piled and dusted. Also, please advise her that stacks of more than 4 have a tendency to tip. May I suggest that my bedroom window sill is not in use and would make an excellent spot for future soap deliveries. One more item. I have purchased another bar of bath-size Dial which I am keeping in the hotel vault in order to avoid future misunderstandings.

     S.Berman

www.ingramcontent.com/pod-product-compliance
Lightning Source LLC
Chambersburg PA
CBHW031625040426

42452CB00007B/678